The Altar: In the Christian Charismatic Church

Chris Legebow

DEDICATION

This book is dedicated to Apostles, Prophets, Evangelists, Pastors, Teachers and other ministry teams that have impacted my life for Christ because of their preaching, teaching, honouring of God with .emphasis on the altar in the Christian Charismatic Church.

CONTENTS

ACKNOWLEDGMENTS

Biblegateway.com (KJV)

INTRODUCTION

THE IMPORTANCE OF THE ALTAR

Most of our Charismatic and Pentecostal churches, the altar is a place on the floor in front of the platform. People gather there to pray. It is more than a place to pray – it is a place of life and death. It is a place of dying to self and saying yes to Christ. It is a place of destiny decisions and we should not make it less important. We should emphasize it's importance in each service. It is not a place you go to once and never again. All the sheep should be making an altar at the altar each week. It is a place where the Word of God is confirmed in us and impartations are received. There are altar prayer workers who can pray with people or people can pray alone. It is a place where the sinner is saved, and the saints present themselves fresh to God.

Abraham met God and established an altar. He built it. He consecrated himself and received from God the words God spoke to him. He did it more than once. Each occasion God spoke to him, Abraham built a new altar. It was a place of accepting and submitting to what God had spoken. Each of these instances marked a change in his life.

Genesis 12: 8 From there he went on toward the hills east of Bethel and pitched his tent, with Bethel on the west and Ai on the east. There he built an altar to the LORD and called on the name of the LORD.

The Charismatic Christian Church

Genesis 13: 18 So Abram went to live near the great trees of Mamre at Hebron, where he pitched his tents. There he built an altar to the LORD.

There was a special altar where God instructed Abraham what to do. He instructed him to sacrifice certain animals and divide their bodies in two. It was a place where God's Holy presence went in between the sacrifice and consecrated it and received it. It was a place of eternal consequence as Abrahamic covenant was established.

Genesis 15: 17 When the sun had set and darkness had fallen, a smoking firepot with a blazing torch appeared and passed between the pieces. 18 On that day the LORD made a covenant with Abram and said, "To your descendants I give this land, from the Wadi[e] of Egypt to the great river, the Euphrates— 19 the land of the Kenites, Kenizzites, Kadmonites, 20 Hittites,Perizzites, Rephaites, 21 Amorit es, Canaanites, Girgashites and Jebusites."

Jacob built an altar after his speaking with God. It was a destiny decision. He chose to follow God with all his life.
Genesis 35: 14 Jacob set up a stone pillar at the place where God had talked with him, and he poured out a drink offering on it; he also poured oil on it.15 Jacob called the place where God had talked with him Bethel.
Abraham built altars after God speaking with him. They were places of confirmation: receiving from God and offering a sacrifice of praise.

King David had sinned and because of it all of Israel was suffering from a plague. David begged God for a solution as he knew it was his fault and he didn't want more people to die. He went to the spot God directed him to and he built an altar there. It had consequences immediately – the plague was stopped. God received the sacrifice as an atonement.
David built an altar

1 Chronicles 21: 18 Then the angel of the LORD ordered Gad to tell David to go up and build an altar to the LORD on the threshing floor of Araunah the Jebusite.19 So David went up in obedience to the word that Gad had spoken in the name of the LORD.

2 Samuel 24: 25 David built an altar to the LORD there and sacrificed burnt offerings and fellowship offerings. Then the LORD answered his prayer in behalf of the land, and the plague on Israel was stopped.

Moses built an altar after a tremendous defeating of the enemy. He did it to honour God giving Him glory.
The Charismatic Christian Church
Exodus 17: 15 Moses built an altar and called it The LORD is my Banner. 16 He said, "Because hands were lifted up against[c] the throne of the LORD,[d] the LORD will be at war against the Amalekites from generation to generation."

Later God established "the altar" as a necessary part of worship of God. He instructed Moses how to build it and gave instruction, so the priests could use it. It was a place where the blood of animals was offered for human sin. It could not erase the sin, but it was a place of atonement. God accepted the sacrifice until Jesus came and shed his blood for us to erase – all sin and iniquity to those who believe on him (1 John 1: 7).

Judaism is not man's religion of how to serve God; it is direct obedience to God's instructions to the prophets. Judaism was started by God communicating with man. The Mosaic altar was established by God. God gave instruction on the size, shape dimensions as well as the offerings. Exodus 27: 1- 8   God instructed Moses on how to build an altar for sacrifice. Sheep, rams, bulls, doves established as sacrifices as burnt offerings.

Solomon establishes an altar at the Temple

King David desired to build a temple for God, but God wouldn't let him, so David got the plans for how to build it and gathered all the materials and finances knowing that his son Solomon would do it. The altar was necessary in the Old Testament because people couldn't approach God directly, or they would die because God is Holy and people are not. The altar was a place to offer a sin offering, or a thanksgiving offering etc. 2 Chronicles 1: 5 But the bronze altar that Bezalel son of Uri, the son of Hur, had made was in Gibeon in front of the tabernacle of the LORD; so Solomon and the assembly inquired of him there. 6 Solomon went up to the bronze altar before the LORD in the tent of meeting and offered a thousand burnt offerings on it.

New Testament Altar

In the New Testament we receive Jesus shed blood at Calvary for our sins. We receive it once and we become Christians. Should we sin, we make an altar quickly: we repent, accept Jesus shed blood and accept forgiveness of sins. There are many opportunities for such altars. They are destiny decision places. Because Christ lives in us in the person of the Holy Spirit, we can pray constantly and in any place. We can repent, praise, worship any place we go. How much so more important is the place of the altar in our congregations. It can be gathering at the front of the church, but it can also be praying at your seats. It can be kneeling or standing. It is a spiritual posture of receiving from God. It is a place of giving of all of oneself to God. We offer ourselves as a living sacrifice to God (Romans 12: 1-2).

The Charismatic Christian Church

Hebrews 9: 14 How much more, then, will the blood of Christ, who through the eternal Spirit offered himself unblemished to God, cleanse our consciences from acts that lead to death, so that we may serve the living God!

The Significance of the Altar

The altar is a place of sacrifice. We are the sacrifice. We repent, receive blessings, receive strength, healing, promises from God etc. The preaching of the Word is received in our hearts and we are changed by our coming to the altar. It is a destiny decision place of accepting new truths and recommitting our lives. It is of most importance in our gatherings. There should always be an opportunity to honour God by going forward for prayer, praise, worship, etc.

The altar call should be specific also. There should be some place to receive the truths taught that day in the service. There should be a place of decision where the saints can step forward not only with their bodies but in their hearts move closer to God. The confirming of truths, things settled – resolved – permanence of decisions there are matters of eternity. Life changing destiny decisions are made at the altar: salvation, healing, deliverance, consecration, thanksgiving, accepting God's instructions/God's Word, marriage, baby dedication, confirmation, prayer and impartation from others, prophecy, commissioning etc.

Preaching God's Word

The Word of God should always be two-way communication: the giving of the word by the pastor or leader and the receiving of the word by the congregation. An altar call is necessary. It is the place of receiving. It can be short or long but the moving of one's body for the purpose of confirming the truth is often necessary. You could make an altar at your seat, or you could go to the front of the church. Your making of an altar is a willful decision to put God first. It is a place of consecration.
Prayer at the altar-is an outward representation of a deep spiritual inner work.

Chapter   Study Questions
Your answers can be brief or long – you determine the effort you put into the answering of the questions. It is meant to be a type of devotional examination of your own Christian life experience in church.

1. Describe the role of an altar in your life. Give testimony of at least 3 occasions it changed your life.
2. Have you yourself ministered at the altar? Describe your role and the importance of the anointing, the gifts of the Holy Spirit and the study of God's Word during your ministry.
3. In your goal of ministry, how can you add in an altar aspect so those receiving always get a chance to draw closer to God?
 4. Describe your daily life devotions. Is there always an altar?

1 THE ALTAR: LIFE CHOICES

Salvation

At some point in your life, you either made the decision to receive Christ or shall make the decision to receive Jesus Christ as your Saviour. It could be in a church sanctuary or it could be in a special evangelical service or in your home. It can occur with others directing you to pray or yourself realizing that Jesus is God. The decision to receive Christ is a destiny decision of eternal significance. Choosing Jesus Christ means you will never die. You will live with Christ ruling and reigning with Him. It can occur anywhere at anytime. It is the Holy Spirit that draws us to Christ. Christians may witness to you – that is share Christ with you, but you must make the decision. So important is that first prayer asking Jesus to cleanse you live in your spirit and be your Saviour and Lord. The altar workers who pray must be tender hearted, gentle, and discerning. God can quicken scriptures to them so they can pray most effectively for the person. These scriptures are some of the scriptures that can be used to share Christ with others.

Rom 10: 13

Whosoever calls upon the name of the LORD shall be saved

Romans 10: 9

If you believe in your heart and confess with your mouth that Jesus Christ is Lord you shall be saved.

John 3: [15] That whosoever believeth in him should not perish, but have eternal life.

[16] For God so loved the world, that he gave his only begotten Son, that whosoever believeth in him should not perish, but have everlasting life.

[17] For God sent not his Son into the world to condemn the world; but that the world through him might be saved.

John 11: [25] Jesus said unto her, I am the resurrection, and the life: he that believeth in me, though he were dead, yet shall he live:

True Altar

The true altar is the heart of each person. It is a heart attitude towards God – keeping the heart tender soft – towards God. Sin separates a person from God. Keeping right with God means being quick to repent, humble, prayerful and totally reliant on Jesus Christ. It means letting the Holy Spirit lead and guide you – obeying the prompting of the Spirit.

The Holy Spirit nudges a person in the spirit – it is comparable to a physical nudge in the body. The person is aware it is there. As we obey these promptings, the Holy Spirit leads the person in the Spirit. This is called walking in the Spirit as well as living in the Spirit. It is the ability to live the scriptures. It is the ability to keep God's Word as priority in all decision making.

Ezekiel 36: [26] A new heart also will I give you, and a new spirit will I put within you: and I will take away the stony heart out of your flesh, and I will give you an heart of flesh.

[27] And I will put my spirit within you, and cause you to walk in my statutes, and ye shall keep my judgments, and do them.

Ez 11: [19] And I will give them one heart, and I will put a new spirit within you; and I will take the stony heart out of their flesh, and will give them an heart of flesh:

[20] That they may walk in my statutes, and keep mine ordinances, and do them: and they shall be my people, and I will be their God.

Crusades

Evangelists hold special gatherings called crusades. They are campaigns to win souls, bring healing, deliverance and blessings to those who attend. Almost always thousands of people, often millions of people (overseas) are in attendance.

The gift of faith is strong in these meetings to receive Christ – there are manifestations of healings, working of miracles and deliverance – there may be some type of altar call but rarely is everyone ministered to one on one – it is the gift of faith that draws the people – manifestations of the glory of God. It is the preached Word that ignites faith in the hearts of the people. They are quickened by the hearing of God's Word responding by receiving their healing or miracle.

Although there is not often person to person ministry in crusades of thousands and hundreds of thousands of people, there is always a strong excellent preaching of God's Word with miracles, signs and wonders following. There are always non-Christians present in these conferences who come so they can be healed. Many of them come, are healed, receive salvation and their lives are radically changed. Often people answer altar calls by taking a step of faith because the altar area is so packed with people not everyone can enter it.

The largest Crusade I've been personally a part of was approximately 20, 000 people. It was in North America. The atmosphere was worship, praise, healings, miracles. It was hours and hours long. No one wanted to leave. The preaching itself was approximately 40 min. but the ministry of prayer and prophetic word went on and on for hours. The atmosphere is glorious. No one wants to leave.

Twenty thousand people gathered to worship Jesus is a huge number for many to grasp but in other nations, people travel to go to Crusades. In Africa there are Crusades of hundreds of thousands and millions of people. They broadcast with huge screens and speakers. People walk for days to attend. They expect a miracle. Often, they receive it. Reinhardt Bonnke, an International Evangelist that passed away in 2020, had a dream to preach Christ to all of Africa. For decades he held huge Crusades with healings, salvation, deliverance and a documented case with DVD evidence of a pastor who had died and four days later he was resurrected from the dead. In his meetings, the preaching would be short – always a salvation message with scripture – sometimes an emphasis on certain types of healing or deliverance. The worship, the ministry would go on all day into the late evening.

Conferences

Teaching conferences of particular topic or to a specific group of Christians are sometimes in the thousands but can be smaller. Some rededicate their lives, some receive Christ – there is some spiritual dynamic to the gathering of saints

Conferences are teaching ministries of Christian truths. There are some huge gatherings of thousands but often there is a teaching atmosphere and some type of refreshment so people can converse with each other. I've been to large conferences of 20, 000. I've been to conference of hundreds. The atmosphere is different than that of a Crusade. There are Christians gathered to receive instruction, training and equipping. The altar calls are prayerful acceptance of God's Word into their spirit. The prayers are important. The atmosphere is one of learning Christian truths so that one can minister to someone else.

Concerts
The music as well as the lyrics and Surrounding Christians compel people to accept Christ or strengthens Christians.

I started going to Christian concerts as soon as I became a Christian. Music was always important in my life. I started going to secular concerts at the age of 11 and continued going to all types of concerts until I became a Christian. Christian concerts are exciting because there is always excellent music, worship, and often a Christian message whether brief or long. The atmosphere can be exciting, dynamic, energetic with dancing, worshipful and prayerful. The prayer is often at your seat – but it is not unimportant. A true Christian concert is more than listening to music – it is a spiritual experience. It isn't just the lyrics, but the focus is on Christ.
Matthew 18: 19 Again I say unto you, That if two of you shall agree on earth as touching any thing that they shall ask, it shall be done for them of my Father which is in heaven.

20 For where two or three are gathered together in my name, there am I in the midst of them.

Church services
In some churches there are special services where there are occasions to bring visitors such as concerts or drams or evangelistic events or movies etc. Whether or not there are these special opportunities visitors are always welcome to attend. It is the Holy Spirit that draws the people unto Christ (John 6: 44).

I did not become a Christian until I was 21. I accepted Christ in a friend's home. I was radically changed inwardly and my lifestyle followed. I wanted to go to Church, in a miracle. I began attending Church. I was brought to a place of prayer, praise, worship, preaching, teaching, as well as being a place of approximately 2,500 members. I was immersed in a Christian atmosphere which was the best thing that could have occurred. I learned how to pray by going to the altar calls after each service. I didn't go because someone told me to go or out of any other reason but the prompting of the Holy Spirit drawing me to go to the front of the Church, kneel pray. There was a wooden altar there. Ministers and altar counsellors would come pray for those at the front. Often most of the church went forward, so one couldn't get to the front unless sitting in the first row.

There was always preservice prayer and respect for God in the sanctuary – it was almost always a silent or whisper experience on Sundays. People who wanted to talk, stayed in the hallways, drank coffee and spoke to each other there. I went to the altar so I could receive the Words of life that were preached or taught. I had no religious hangups or resistance because I was sincerely a new Christian receiving God's Word as truth. I took Bible classes there with hundreds of people. I was established in the Christian faith because of the balanced preaching and teaching of God's Word.

The other churches in my life did not have a structural altar but rather a metaphorical one – an open place at the front of the church where people would kneel and pray. Some of the churches I attended the altar call meant dancing and shouting, laughing, crying etc. No one orchestrated it except the Holy Spirit. Often the ministers would pray for people, and sometimes we, the congregation, prayed for each other. There was freedom to linger in prayer or leave. It should never be automatic or like a factory. I've visited some churches where it is that. It is not the type of altar I am speaking of. Quick one, two second prayer and anointing with oil may serve some useful purpose but it is not the type of prayer and ministry I am referring to – ritual is not the same as a true altar experience. True prayer is speaking to God, in consecration. It may be short. It may be long. It should be personal. Each person should have the freedom to stay and keep praying, even after he or she has been prayed for.

Ephesians 5: [23] And the very God of peace sanctify you wholly; and I pray God your whole spirit and soul and body be preserved blameless unto the coming of our Lord Jesus Christ.

Although there were occasions when we the congregation prayed for each other, Sundays were almost always ministers or prayer counsellors praying for those who went forward. Prayer workers at the altar should always be prepared to minister salvation, healing, deliverance. In the churches that have been in my life, all of them required the altar ministers to get some type of training course. We were given materials such as salvation follow up booklets, anointing oil, new testaments to give to those accepting Christ. We were in agreement with the ministry because we were taught what we should do. The altar prayer team should be equipped, trained, mature Christians who use the gifts of the Holy Spirit as well as the Word of God.

Praying the salvation prayer with someone is one of the most exciting things in a Christian's life. The Christian ministering is sharing Christ with someone whose heart has become soft towards God. He or she is ready to receive Jesus Christ as Saviour and Lord. The message of salvation should be simple. There is no magic formula. It almost always contains these parts: You are a sinner - not able to help yourself. The measure is in keeping the commandments of God as given to Moses.

1 John 1: [7] But if we walk in the light, as he is in the light, we have fellowship one with another, and the blood of Jesus Christ his Son cleanseth us from all sin.

Jesus is the Saviour – He shed his blood so all can be saved

Receiving Jesus Christ's atonement for your life.

Romans 10: [9] That if thou shalt confess with thy mouth the Lord Jesus, and shalt believe in thine heart that God hath raised him from the dead, thou shalt be saved.

John 1: [12] But as many as received him, to them gave he power to become the sons of God, even to them that believe on his name:

[13] Which were born, not of blood, nor of the will of the flesh, nor of the will of man, but of God.

Romans 10: [3] For whosoever shall call upon the name of the Lord shall be saved.

Receiving Christ should be emphasized as important. It is not casual. It is a major decision – a commitment – a consecration a new life in Christ begins as you accept Christ. The altar worker should not only pray – but direct the believer to begin reading the Bible, attend church, etc. Many large churches have a follow up package which is instructions for a New Christian. Many smaller churches do not. The altar worker must point the New Christian in the direction of Christian lifestyle. In North America, there are many people who are not taught the Bible or Christian values unless their parents were Christians. They do not know a Christian lifestyle. It may be a brief prompting of direction but it is necessary.

A salvation prayer can be anywhere at anytime. I know that Gloria Copeland prayed " God, if you can do anything with my life – here it is." It was a simple true giving of her heart to Christ in response to a preached message. The other teaching came later.

The thief on the cross died with Jesus but at his death he prayed a simple prayer (Luke 23: 42) " when you come into your kingdom [Jesus – my emphasis] remember me".

Some people have prayed simple prayers such as " Jesus save me" or "God save me" Theologically it is not correct. Jesus died over 2, 000 years ago. He died once for all. He saved us over 2, 000 years ago. There is no fresh blood flowing to save you, but there is an acceptance of what he accomplished by his death, burial and resurrection. Theologically we accept and apply the blood of Jesus to our lives by faith. Religious people might not like those simple prayers – but God accepts true prayer from the heart.

Chapter 1   questions
1. Write your testimony of salvation. Describe the atmosphere. Describe your spiritual attitude as well as your decision.
2. Was there immediate change in your life at salvation? Write describing at least 3 life changes.
3. If you have not yet made the decision to receive Christ or know that you are not where you should be with Christ, please pray this prayer – in your own words so that your own ears can hear your voice. You can add in your own specifics.

PRAYER FOR SALVATION   Thank you- Jesus that you died for me on the cross. Thank you that you rose from the dead and ascended into heaven. Thank you that you are coming back again. I thank you Jesus for forgiving my sins. Thank you for your blood that cleanses me from all sin and unrighteousness. Thank you that your blood makes me holy. Thank you for saving me. Fill me with the Holy Spirit to overflowing. I pray for the baptism of the Holy Spirit. Lead me to other people who love you and serve you and that can help me know more about you. Give me the discerning of spirits strong. I thank you and praise you. With my mouth, I confess Jesus Christ is my LORD. Amen.

Prayer of Rededication
Jesus, I repent from the way I've been living. I claim your precious blood over my life. I receive the cleansing of your blood. Strengthen me so I can live in the freedom of Christ. Holy Spirit, lead me. Quicken scriptures to me. I thank you for freedom. I determine to live my life honouring you. Amen.

You should get the communion elements and take communion with God's presence. Worship, praise and receive strength. Use 1 Cor 11: 23-31 as a guide or your own scriptures.

2 MINISTERING AT THE ALTAR

As an Altar counsellor I was first equipped with and excellent resource that I highly recommend to all churches or ministries. A 700 club prayer team manual – scripture references – anointing oil.

Pastors should also engage in praying for the people. It is a way of knowing the people and ministering personally to them. In large churches, often the pastors don't get to know each person n the congregation unless he or she makes an effort. One way of getting close to the congregation is to pray over them as part of a ministry team.

John 10: 10 : I am come so that they might have life and more abundantly."

The Good Shepherd – Jesus is our example. He cares for us corporately but also as individuals. Jesus lived with the disciples for 3 years teaching, ministering etc. with them as family. He had compassion on those who he taught – thousands of people would gather to listen to his preaching. He fed the 5, 000 because he had compassion on them. He sincerely cared for their well being. The pastors and church leaders and ministers must have the same kind of care for the congregation. God gives severe warnings to Christian leaders who do not care for the sheep.

In Ezekiel 34, God gives warning to the shepherds who do not care for the sheep. The metaphor of Shepherd as leader or minister of God's people is used throughout the Bible. A Shepherd must keep the sheep together so they are not scattered. Their strength is with the Shepherd; should they go astray, they can be wounded or prey to wolves or lions etc. Ezekiel was prophesying over the evil shepherds who abused the sheep. He was speaking words of judgement over them.

Ezekiel 34: [3] Ye eat the fat, and ye clothe you with the wool, ye kill them that are fed: but ye feed not the flock.

[4] The diseased have ye not strengthened, neither have ye healed that which was sick, neither have ye bound up that which was broken, neither have ye brought again that which was driven away, neither have ye sought that which was lost; but with force and with cruelty have ye ruled them.

[5] And they were scattered, because there is no shepherd: and they became meat to all the beasts of the field, when they were scattered.

[6] My sheep wandered through all the mountains, and upon every high hill: yea, my flock was scattered upon all the face of the earth, and none did search or seek after them.

The opposite of a Shepherd that abuses the sheep or neglects them is someone who strengthens the sheep, feeds the sheep, applies oil and wine – to the wounds to bring healing to the sheep; a true shepherd keeps track of the number of sheep and where they are. It is essential that he or she not lose any of them. If there is a lost sheep, the shepherd seeks it out because sheep cannot care for themselves or protect themselves. The ministers of the church, altar prayer counsellors should pray for each person as though it were the most important person. It is essential true-life giving ministry be imparted at the altar.

God can use the giftings of the Holy Spirit through the ministry team as they pray over the sheep. Often the people will pray things that are as special ointment to comfort, heal or bless the sheep. Most often it is scripture or scriptures. The pastors as well as elders, deacons and prayer team assist each other and are a strength to the Church as they minister together. Most large churches have scripture references for altar workers. Smaller churches often do not. As training for altar workers there should be scripture references for various topics of prayer. These booklets or books are not expensive and are vital to give accurate scriptures to the person praying. The alternative to getting them as a church is to create your own reference list covering main topics of prayer.

Praying the Scriptures over a person is sowing God's Word into that person's life. God's Word will not return void but it will accomplish and prosper in the thing it is sent to do (Isaiah 55: 11)

Healing

Ministering healing should be a part of our usual prayer at the altar. We must have faith to believe as well as receive the ministering of healing. Our altar workers must know the scriptures on healing and believe that Jesus is living in them as they minister healing. Faith is the essential aspect. The person receiving must believe he or she can receive healing. The presence of God can be strong or not. God honours His Word. That is why the praying of scripture over a person is so important.

Healing (this portion is from my book Sacraments: a Charismatic Guide)

There are many occasions where the disciples laid hands on the sick and they were healed. It was not simply an outward action; it was an impartation of faith for healing. As Paul and his companions were ship wreaked, they came to an Island – it was Malta. Paul lays hands and prays for a person and he is healed.

Acts 28: 8 It happened that the father of Publius lay sick with a fever and dysentery. Paul visited him and, placing his hands on him, prayed and healed him. 9 When this happened, the rest on the island who had diseases also came and were healed.

Our churches should practice the laying on of hands for healing. Often, they will anoint with oil and pray for healing. Believing elders and ministry are often the ones who do it; sometimes altar prayer workers do it. We should offer this sacrament each week so that people who are in need of healing will be able to come. It should be preached from the pulpit regularly so people who are new or who are visiting can get the truth that Jesus Christ is the healer.

Hebrews 13: 8 Jesus Christ is the same yesterday, and today, and forever.
We should be teaching and practicing what the Word of God promises us. Jesus who died for our sins, also took upon Himself all the curses of the law from Deuteronomy 28. The Messiah would fulfill the promises of Isaiah. Jesus Christ is the Messiah.

Isaiah 53: 5 But he was wounded for our transgressions, he was bruised for our iniquities; the chastisement of our peace was upon him, and by his stripes we are healed

The words "by his stripes we are healed" means salvation but also physical healing. The Apostle Peter uses these exact words to minister healing (2 Peter 2: 24). It is so important that we pray for one another so there will be no sick among us.

Some people believe the lie that God places sickness on people to teach them or mature them. This is a direct lie that contradicts God 's words. Sickness was named as a curse of sin. God called it a curse. He most certainly would not use a curse to teach one of his children. The truth is some people have not read all of God's Word so if they hear a minister say such a thing as God is in it or some such language, they don't know there is healing. They don't know God.

Deuteronomy 28: 61 Also every sickness and every plague which is not written in the Book of the Law will the Lord bring upon you until you are destroyed.

The blessing of God is on those who serve God and honour Him. If that was true in the Mosaic covenant, it most certainly is true in the covenant of Jesus Christ who paid the full ransom for our lives with his life. Jesus helped show himself as Messiah by healing multitudes of people. If it was God's will to use sickness for those people, Jesus never would have healed them. The good news of the gospel of Jesus Christ means that you can be healed in spirit, soul and body.

Acts 10: 38 how God anointed Jesus of Nazareth with the Holy Spirit and with power, who went about doing good and healing all who were oppressed by the devil, for God was with Him.

Please notice God's Word says the sickness "oppressed by the devil" not a blessing of God.

In Matthew it states the following:
Matthew 12: 15 But when Jesus knew it, He withdrew from there. And great crowds followed Him, and He healed them all.

Since sickness is a curse not a blessing, people may foolishly believe that sickness is a direct result of sin. This is not true. Even the disciples believed that perhaps this was always true. Jesus corrects his disciples and heals the man and clearly says it was not because of sin and he showed God's will to heal.

John 9: 1As Jesus passed by, He saw a man blind from birth. 2 His disciples asked Him, "Rabbi, who sinned, this man or his parents, that he was born blind?"
3 Jesus answered, "Neither this man nor his parents sinned. But it happened so that the works of God might be displayed in him. 4 I must do the works of Him who sent Me while it is day. Night is coming when no one can work. 5 While I am in the world, I am the light of the world."

There are many excellent books on healing and receiving healing. If this is new information to you, please get yourself some Christian materials on healing. There are many present-day healing evangelists such as Oral Roberts, Gloria Copeland, Kenneth Copeland, Marilyn Hickey, Benny Hinn etc. I give you these names because all of them preach Jesus Christ the healer.

Healing comes through faith in Jesus Christ. Faith comes through the hearing of God's Word. It is essential for you to get scriptures about healing into your spirit. Get the scriptures into you by reading them out loud, hearing them and confessing them with your mouth. Reading the Bible and getting God's Word into you is essential for you to be proactive – get the scripture in you so that should something occur and sickness come, you can speak God's word over it and drive it out.

Results of the curse of sin

Sickness, disease, pestilence, hatred, wars, envy, strife – all these things are a result of the curse. Because Adam and Eve sinned, these things exist in our world. You may think God doesn't heal everyone. Please know that if a person is not healed – it is not God who choose to kill him or her. It is essential that we have faith in God's Word yes; it must be on the inside of our innermost being. It is also necessary for us to be wise stewards of our earthly bodies. Please note what we put in to our body directly effects our health.

The Body a Temple

In our modern North American Culture, we often dine on fast food – mostly greasy and salty and high in calories. A can of pop or soda is often 800 calories. A burger sometimes 1,000. Calories. An average person should get 2,500 – 3,000 Calories a day. Junk food –lives up to its name. Chocolate bars, chips, candy – thousands of calories. Please do not pump these things into your body constantly and expect to be healthy. It matters what we put in. I don't pretend to be a dietician, but I made some healthy food choices in my life several years ago because I want to live as long as I can.

1 Corinthians 6: 19 What? Do you not know that your body is the temple of the Holy Spirit, who is in you, whom you have received from God, and that you are not your own? 20 You were bought with a price. Therefore glorify God in your body and in your spirit, which are God's.

Through my explanation, please see that is God's desire for people to live long and be healthy. Also, each person must make wise healthy choices and teach his or her children etc. I have heard of, not witnessed, a miracle of weight loss. Someone overly obese who went for prayer because of all the health issues that arose because of obesity. Although the person was miraculously healed, the person went back to his or her poor habits and became ill once more.

Gloria Copland has an excellent book: Living Long: Finish Strong. It talks about this subject from a Christian point of view. Don't believe the lie that you have to die of a certain disease because it runs in your family. Don't believe the lie that you will die at an early age because others in your family did. Yes we inherit some things from our families, but we can make a difference by doing our part both spiritually building up your faith and naturally by caring for our bodies.

Read the scriptures about healing. Do your part to be healthy but should there be sickness, most certainly get prayer for healing by someone with faith in Jesus the healer.

Matthew 18: 19 "Again I say to you, that if two of you agree on earth about anything they ask, it will be done for them by My Father who is in heaven. 20 For where two or three are assembled in My name, there I am in their midst."

Literally as we pray for each other, Jesus Christ is in the midst of us and His presence can bring healing. The healing can be immediate or gradual. God also gifts doctors and health care professionals to use their skills to help save lives. I have received healing in all these ways. I give God the glory.

Immediate healing
I was not feeling well. I was ill. I believed I could not go to church. My friend came to pick me up as he usually did. I shared with him. He laid hands on me and prayed for me and I was immediately healed. I was able to go to church. It was instant.

Gradual Healing
I have been healed with gradual healing. I was very ill coughing etc. It was hard to breath etc. I read the scriptures to myself. I went to church knowing that they would pray for the sick. I went forward to a minister I knew believing in divine healing. She anointed me with oil and prayed a short prayer over me. I felt God's power go right through the top of my head. I don't know if I expected a longer more awesome prayer or what but as I walked I didn't notice any difference. I shared with my friends that I would have to go home because I wasn't well enough to go out. I believe they were both praying for me. They didn't say they were but I believe it. As I was on my way driving towards home, it suddenly dawned on me; I was breathing normally. I wasn't coughing. I felt excellent. I was healed. I shared it with them and we did our usual special Sunday dinner.

Anointing with oil
James 5: 14 Is anyone sick among you? Let him call for the elders of the church, and let them pray over him, anointing him with oil in the name of the Lord. 15 And the prayer of faith will save the sick, and the Lord will raise him up. And if he has committed any sins, he will be forgiven.

The Bible clearly instructs us what to do if we are ill. We should get elders or ministers to pray the prayer of faith over us for healing anointing us with oil. Oil is only a symbol of the Holy Spirit. There is no special magic about the oil. It is a symbol of God's presence. It reminds the person praying and the receiver to believe for the manifest healing presence of God.

This scripture covers various things. I want to discuss each of them so that your faith rises up for each of them.

1. Call for the elders – if you cannot get to church, phone and ask someone to come pray for you. You must make a contact with somebody who can pray. You must realize God wants you healthy. Often, I have not only contacted my local church but ministries that I support because they pray and believe for healing.

2. Anoint with oil in the name of the LORD – The LORD Jesus Christ – anointing with oil is what God commanded we do; we should obey. The oil is a symbol but God said to do it so we should do it.

3. The prayer of faith will heal the sick. Usually, the ill person needs a boost of faith by someone who is healthy and believes God's Word. It can be the person's own faith; it can be the faith of the minister. Faith must be present. You cannot pray unscriptural prayers like "If it be your will to heal O God…" and expect results. You will not find a prayer like it in the Bible anywhere. In Luke 5: 12 a leper says those words to Jesus and Jesus says I will heal you. Jesus heals him. A prayer of faith involves praying the scriptures over a person with true faith that impartation for healing is present.

4. And if he has committed any sins – if the sickness comes because of sin or disobedience to God either neglecting your body or living outside of God's commandments – that is the realm of the curse. God promises, even if the person has sinned, he or she will be forgive as he or she comes for anointing with oil and the healing prayer of faith.

This specific points should comfort any person because God has made provision in this sacrament that you might be healed: spirit, soul and body.

Healing in the soul of a Person

Often people who have experienced the death of a loved one or a divorce or other such tragedy will be overcome with grief. It is normal to grieve the loss of a loved one but we as Christians do not grieve as the world grieves (1 Thessalonians 4: 13). The person who has become wounded in his or her spirit and is overcome with grief not only needs prayer but needs inner healing. Please know the lie that says that healing of such matters comes as years go by. Life may continue but healing doesn't naturally come to a deep wounded in the spirit. The soul of a person is the mind, will and emotions. It is at this level that grief comes. If you are strong in spirit, you can heal in soul. You will overcome the situation.

This is good news for anyone that came from a home where there was abuse or neglect or anything less than a Christian loving family. You don't have to remain a victim. You may have been abused physically, verbally or sexually. You do not have to remain a victim all your life. Do not be given over to self-absorption. If you focus on yourself and what was done to you and why it is unfair etc. you will stay a victim for the remainder of your life. I know it sounds like harsh words, but if you know you are not happy with your life and you are thinking about how you were wounded or you can't see past the divorce or the death, you are in need of healing for your soul. Living in the realm of the soul is never the best for a Christian and it can lead to a wounded spirit.

Galatians 5: 16 I say then, walk in the Spirit, and you shall not fulfill the lust of the flesh.
Galatians 5: 25 If we live in the Spirit, let us also walk in the Spirit.

God wants us to live in the spirit and constantly renew our strength in the Holy Spirit. A broken spirit can occur when a person is constantly living in the soulish realm absorbed with what was done to him or her. This type of person cannot talk about anything without being negative. This type of person is like a black hole to anyone close to him or her. That is the person dumps negative stuff into the atmosphere around him or her. It is not a lack of compassion that causes me to say this. In fact, it is of understanding and compassion of God that compels me to say, no one has to live a victim of life. There is hope in Jesus Christ for healing of your soul.

Isaiah 53: 4 Surely he has borne our grief and carried our sorrows; Yet we esteemed him stricken, smitten of God, and afflicted. 5 But he was wounded for our transgressions, he was bruised for our iniquities; the chastisement of our peace was upon him, and by his stripes we are healed.

Mere positive thinking will not help a person wounded in the spirit. The person needs deep inner healing of the soul and possibly deliverance of an evil spirit of depression. The good news is that Jesus died for our sins and iniquities and our physical healing but also for our soul. He gave his life as a handsome for our souls. There is provision in the blood of Jesus and in the resurrected LORD for complete and total healing. Jesus took upon himself "the chastisement of our peace" that means he took the curse of all the negative stuff that could ever wound you or I and the curse of it died with Christ; Jesus rose from the dead in triumph over all things of the earth and the curse.

If this describes you or someone close to you, pray for the person yes, but the Word of God must be ministered to the person so he or she knows the truth of Jesus triumph.

John 8: 32 "You shall know the truth, and the truth shall set you free."
Romans 10: 17 So then faith comes by hearing, and hearing by the word of God.

The person should get faith teaching on the healing of the soul. Joyce Meyer has a strong testimony of complete and total healing and is a living example of this truth that Christ can take a broken person and completely heal and anoint and give new hope and life to a person. She has excellent books and teaching on beauty for ashes, and these topics. I highly recommend her CDs and books be shared with the person in need of inner healing. I have personally known of many people who were transformed by her testimony and her teachings. Once the person acknowledges he or she needs inner healing, the person should get prayer and anointing with oil from a minister of the gospel who believes that Jesus can heal the soul of a person.

I have experienced complete and total healing of my soul. I didn't even know what was going on. I didn't even know about my spiritual condition. I was a Christian, desiring to know God more. At first, I realized I had to come into agreement with God's Word and what God said about me. I started praying and confessing what God says about me. I began to notice my words more and more. The Holy Spirit was so gentle with me, leading me so that I could be transformed and know life beyond any joy I ever knew about. I prayed

Psalm 19: 14 Let the words of my mouth and the meditation of my heart be acceptable in Your sight, O Lord, my strength and my Redeemer.

Words we speak

I heard Gloria Copeland preach on God correcting us if we let Him. If we pray " Holy Spirit , please correct my mouth if my words do line up with your word." I prayed it and God started correcting me. If I said something insulting about myself or others, God checked me. Don't say negative things about yourself. You have to live with yourself always. Start saying I can do all things through Christ who strengthens me. Get the word "I can't" out of your vocabulary.

What we Think About

What we think about matters. We can change how we feel depending on what we listen to or what we watch or what we hear. That is why it is so important to get teachings and scriptures to listen to. It is important to watch things that are pure. It is important to think about God's Word and what He says about us in His Word. For instance, God says we are more than conquerors in Christ Jesus. Guard your heart. Keep yourself wholly fixed on

God and do not believe anything that goes against what God says in His Word.

Philippians 4: 8 Finally, brothers, whatever things are true, whatever things are honest, whatever things are just, whatever things are pure, whatever things are lovely, whatever things are of good report, if there is any virtue, and if there is any praise, think on these things.
Romans 8: 37 No, in all these things we are more than conquerors through Him who loved us.

Who we are With

Being with someone rather than alone is not always the answer to loneliness. A person who does not build you up spiritually and encourage you with scripture is not someone who can make a difference in your life positively. If the person is not encouraging you spiritually – be alone with God reading the scriptures, listening to them and saying them so your own ears can hear you speak them. What you say about yourself matters the most. If you can get your words in alignment with God's Word, you will start seeing a difference in your life. God will bring Christian friends in your life who will encourage you and strengthen and build you up. Until that occurs, keep constantly build up your own self with psalms and hymns and spiritual songs and scriptures (Ephesians 5: 19).

Jude 1: 20 But you, beloved, build yourselves up in your most holy faith. Pray in the Holy Spirit. 21 Keep yourselves in the love of God while you are waiting for the mercy of our Lord Jesus Christ, which leads to eternal life.

What we do

Give and it shall be given unto you (Luke 6: 38). I know it can mean finances but it can also be a principal of all of life in the spirit. Start serving others. Start giving of yourself to care for others. If you can, get active in your local church by serving or baking at dinners. You could volunteer to start ministering with the Nursing Home Ministries, or teaching a Sunday school class. The principle of the kingdom of God is to give so that you may receive.

I knew of an elderly widow who not only attended all the churches prayer meetings to pray for others but also gave her home life to prayer and intercession for people, for the church for her family etc. If she got a word of God for you in prayer, it most certainly was something to cherish and pray about because she spent most of her life in prayer.

I remember how the more got involved in Church giving, the more I thought about others and less about myself. I saw people in nursing homes, who were dying and who received a bit of joy as I served communion to them or sang hymns with them. The more you serve others, the less you think about yourself.

Prayer for inner healing
The lie is that depressed people need to think about themselves. Just the opposite is true. Those people need to start caring for others. As they serve and give, God honours them by blessing them in so many ways, physically, financially and spiritually.

Receiving a prayer for inner healing is essential for those who have been wounded by life. It can occur with you and God privately. It can occur with a minister praying for you and anointing you with oil. In order to see a difference in your life, you must make a difference in your life. Start investing the Word of God into your life. Start serving and giving and pursuing God realizing the blessings that God has given to you and becoming thankful. Thank and praise God for what He has done for you. Focus on the blessings not on any negative thing. Focus on the Living Christ who lives in you. If you are living in the Spirit, you cannot live in the flesh. You cannot live in both. Choosing to honour God and to literally believe the Word of God and pray it and confess it and live it – is the answer that can bring a new life. Hebrews 11: 6 But without faith it is impossible to please him: for he that cometh to God must believe that he is, and that he is a rewarder of them that diligently seek him.

Those who minister in prayer must literally believe the following: Mark 16: 17 And these signs shall follow them that believe; In my name shall they cast out devils; they shall speak with new tongues; 18 They shall take up serpents; and if they drink any deadly thing, it shall not hurt them; they shall lay hands on the sick, and they shall recover. The pastors, elders and deacons and altar workers should especially receive training to pray for healing. James 1:13 Is any among you afflicted? let him pray. Is any merry? let him sing psalms. 14 Is any sick among you? let him call for the elders of the church; and let them pray over him, anointing him with oil in the name of the Lord: 15 And the prayer of faith shall save the sick, and the Lord shall raise him up; and if he have committed sins, they shall be forgiven him.

Notice the question. Is there any? Because there shouldn't be normally any sick. God's desire is to prosper us spiritually, physically, financially etc. (Deut. 28: 1- 14)

If there are sick, they should appeal to the leaders, the pastors, the mature (those who know the scriptures as well as believe them) Christians to pray with them for healing.

The prayer for healing involves physical healing as well as healing of the soul and spirit. The altar counsellors must be trained in Christian doctrine.

Healing of the body is available to all people. It is not necessarily only for Christians. Many people that do not know Jesus come to Christian Crusades and healing meetings so they can be healed. They have tried everything else and they have heard that Jesus heals, so they come. Once Christ heals someone, he or she almost always receives Christ as Saviour. Luke 17: 11-19 shares the story of Jesus speaking to lepers to be healed. All of them were healed but one returned to thank Jesus for his healing.

Healing of the soul

The soul is the mind, emotions, will of a person. It is what a person believes about himself/herself or others, his or her experiences, feelings, desires etc. Before a person receives salvation – the person lives in the body and in the soul realm. It means what he or she wants, thinks feels is most important. The spirit is comparable to a wrinkled dry balloon.

Once a person becomes a Christian, the spirit of the person is quickened by the presence of the Holy Spirit who comes to dwell in Christians. Christ lives in us by the miracle of the Holy Spirit indwelling. The person's spirit blooms and is full – as a balloon that has air in it. It is the presence of God. The Christian living in the spirit obeys the promptings of the Holy Spirit. As the Christian reads the Word of God, receives preaching, teaching, worships, prays and soaks in the presence of God, the person is transformed in the soul. The Holy Spirit's fruit becomes a part of the person's identity.

Galatians 5 : [22] But the fruit of the Spirit is love, joy, peace, longsuffering, gentleness, goodness, faith, [23] Meekness, temperance: against such there is no law.

The soul of a person is changed from glory to glory – by the Spirit of God dwelling in us. The more we commune with God the more Christlike a person becomes. There are some healings that occur depending on each person's unique past. Some receive instant healing of some things. Others receive healing in different ways. It is our pressing into Christ that determines how much of Christ we receive. Jesus invites us to come to him; each person can get as much of Christ as he/she desires. It means pressing into Christ with all your heart. It means desiring Christ more than anything. The more you desire God's presence, the deeper your relationship with Christ becomes.

John 7: 37 If any man thirst, let him come unto me, and drink.
2 Corinthians [18] But we all, with open face beholding as in a glass the glory of the Lord, are changed into the same image from glory to glory, even as by the Spirit of the Lord.

Christ came so we could be free to live a holy life. The freedom Christ gives is liberty from sin. We do not have to be addicted to anything or anyone. We can be set free from addictions. Many who come to Christ have addictions with sex, alcohol, drugs or negative self concepts etc. No Christian should be content to let the soul dominate him or her. Healing can come spontaneously through praise, worship, receiving a scripture as a RHEMA Word. These types of miracles occur regularly in Christian's lives. There are occasions a pastor may preach a message, the person will respond to the altar call – receive healing in the soul. Once it occurs, that area of life is settled. Never does the thing bother a person again. It is healing as well as deliverance. Deliverance is being set free from the addiction. Healing is the Holy Spirit releasing the person to live without any stigma.

Do not be content to have areas of your life that cause you pain or addictions. You can be set free from your past; you can live in your spirit in Christ enjoying your life fully without any hinderances. Bad habits can end. New life can begin. Jesus came to bring us life. He fulfilled the Messianic prophecy of Isaiah 61.

The Scripture promises that there is good news – the good news or gospel is that Jesus died for you. You can receive life from Him. You can live with freedom. You do not have to be mourning. You can have joy. Vs. 3 says that "the oil of joy" for sorrow or heaviness. Liberty to the captives is literal. Once bound by addictions or bad habits, the people are free to live life fully enjoying their lives. Healing, deliverance – only by Jesus Christ.

Get free - stay free.

Is 61: 1 The Spirit of the Lord GOD is upon me; because the LORD hath anointed me to preach good tidings unto the meek; he hath sent me to bind up the broken hearted, to proclaim liberty to the captives, and the opening of the prison to them that are bound;

2 To proclaim the acceptable year of the LORD, and the day of vengeance of our God; to comfort all that mourn;

3 To appoint unto them that mourn in Zion, to give unto them beauty for ashes, the oil of joy for mourning, the garment of praise for the spirit of heaviness; that they might be called trees of righteousness, the planting of the LORD, that he might be glorified.

4 And they shall build the old wastes, they shall raise up the former desolations, and they shall repair the waste cities, the desolations of many generations.

I applaud all step programs that assist people in getting free of alcohol or drugs or addictions of any type. But the thing I cannot be content with is they claim that thing as their identity. They proclaim it and embrace it as though that is their life destiny. Jesus Christ can set a person free and the person has no identification with the habit or the wound or the thing of the past. The person is whole. The person is healed. The person is free. I've known so many people who have encountered Jesus Christ, who have given public testimony of how Christ has transformed their lives. I've received healing myself. It comes by the Spirit of God. It is part of the blessing of the covenant of Jesus Christ.

One of my pastors had been an alcoholic and did not serve God, but Jesus revealed himself to him and he was completely transformed. He lived all of his life evangelizing, doing missions, being a pastor, praying, worshipping, with a beautiful family living wholly for God. He had special mercy on those who needed deliverance and healing and could speak to them humbly yet with authority. He discipled many youth and men during my years at our Church. He often would go to the person's home, pray with him, get him involved in church activities, direct him to those who could offer a job. He had the heart of an evangelist and often preached on the main street on bust Friday evenings as people lined up to go to the movies or bars. John 8: 36 Jesus truly set him free. With his freedom, he chose to bring others to freedom by sharing Christ.

Jesus suffered so that we could be set free. He was beaten, bruised, had huge nails pounded through his hands and feet, had a sword thrust into his side. He suffered, died on the cross, was buried, rose from the dead and appeared on the earth for 40 days to many witnesses. Those who believe in Jesus' blood shed for all receive eternal life. Many Christian do not know they can live free because of that same shed blood. The blood saves us, heals us, delivers us, prospers and protects us. The blood of Jesus – is the covenant sacrifice fulfilling the requirement for blood sacrifice.

God revealed himself to Moses and through the commandments, Judaism was birthed. It required yearly blood sacrifices for sin. It was necessary to obey the commandment and offer sheep, bulls, goats, as an offering once a year to atone for one's sins. Jesus blood ended the need for blood sacrifice. Jesus blood washed the sins away once and for all. Hebrews 10: [4] For it is not possible that the blood of bulls and of goats should take away sins. [10] By the which will we are sanctified through the offering of the body of Jesus Christ once for all. [11] And every priest standeth daily ministering and offering oftentimes the same sacrifices, which can never take away sins: [12] But this man, after he had offered one sacrifice for sins for ever, sat down on the right hand of God; By his stipes ye are healed. (Is 53: 3-7, 1 Peter 2: 21-25)

HEALING SCRIPTTURES
    Healing is promised in the scriptures but faith is necessary. Faith is the substance necessary. Faith the size of a mustard seed can move a mountain. But it is essential. It can originate with the person seeking healing, Jesus (The Word of God) the person who is ministering.
Hebrews **11: 1** Now faith is the substance of things hoped for, the evidence of things not seen. [6] But without faith it is impossible to please him: for he that cometh to God must believe that he is, and that he is a rewarder of them that diligently seek him.

JESUS MINISTERED HEALING – THE FAITH TO HEAL FROM JESUS
    In this instance it was Jesus with the healing gifts ministering to Simon's mother. Jesus rebuked the disease with his words – the woman was healed.
Luke 4: [38] And he arose out of the synagogue, and entered into Simon's house. And Simon's wife's mother was taken with a great fever; and they besought him for her.

³⁹ And he stood over her, and rebuked the fever; and it left her: and immediately she arose and ministered unto them.

THE FAITH WITHIN THE PERSON – TO RECEIVE - PERSONAL STANDARD OF FAITH.

In this instance it was the people who believed that could they touch Jesus they could be healed. They believed Jesus was the source of healing.
Matthew 14: ³⁶ And besought him that they might only touch the hem of his garment: and as many as touched were made perfectly whole.
Mark 6: ⁵⁶ And whithersoever he entered, into villages, or cities, or country, they laid the sick in the streets, and besought him that they might touch if it were but the border of his garment: and as many as touched him were made whole.
 Luke 8: ⁴³ And a woman having an issue of blood twelve years, which had spent all her living upon physicians, neither could be healed of any,

⁴⁴ Came behind him, and touched the border of his garment: and immediately her issue of blood stanched.

⁴⁵ And Jesus said, Who touched me? When all denied, Peter and they that were with him said, Master, the multitude throng thee and press thee, and sayest thou, Who touched me?

⁴⁶ And Jesus said, Somebody hath touched me: for I perceive that virtue is gone out of me.

⁴⁷ And when the woman saw that she was not hid, she came trembling, and falling down before him, she declared unto him before all the people for what cause she had touched him, and how she was healed immediately.

⁴⁸ And he said unto her, Daughter, be of good comfort: thy faith hath made thee whole; go in peace.

JESUS SPOKE THE WORD IT BROUGHT HEALING

In this instance the lepers appeared near Jesus – he spoke the Word over them and as they went they were healed.
Luke 17: ¹¹ And it came to pass, as he went to Jerusalem, that he passed through the midst of Samaria and Galilee.

¹² And as he entered into a certain village, there met him ten men that were lepers, which stood afar off:

¹³ And they lifted up their voices, and said, Jesus, Master, have mercy on us.

¹⁴ And when he saw them, he said unto them, Go shew yourselves unto the priests. And it came to pass, that, as they went, they were cleansed.

John 9

In this instance Jesus touched and brought healing. The same God who made Adam from the earth, used earth with spittle (mud) and placed it on the eyes of the blind man.

John 9: 6 When he had thus spoken, he spat on the ground, and made clay of the spittle, and he anointed the eyes of the blind man with the clay,

7 And said unto him, Go, wash in the pool of Siloam, (which is by interpretation, Sent.) He went his way therefore, and washed, and came seeing.

ROMAN CENTURION WHO BELIEVED JESUS COULD SPEAK THE WORD BRING HEALING

In this instance, the Centurion (a Gentile – not part of the Covenant promises for healing) believed in Jesus so much that he asked Jesus to speak the word that it might be accomplished, the healing of his servant.

Matthew 8: 5 And when Jesus was entered into Capernaum, there came unto him a centurion, beseeching him,

6 And saying, Lord, my servant lieth at home sick of the palsy, grievously tormented.

7 And Jesus saith unto him, I will come and heal him.

8 The centurion answered and said, Lord, I am not worthy that thou shouldest come under my roof: but speak the word only, and my servant shall be healed.

9 For I am a man under authority, having soldiers under me: and I say to this man, Go, and he goeth; and to another, Come, and he cometh; and to my servant, Do this, and he doeth it.

10 When Jesus heard it, he marvelled, and said to them that followed, Verily I say unto you, I have not found so great faith, no, not in Israel.

Chapter questions
1. Did you receive healing in body, soul spirit? Describe your experiences. There are many Christians that experienced more than one of each – choose one or write them all. It may be the outline of a book you can write.
2. Describe the healing specifically. Did your condition change immediately?
3. Which of the types of ministry healing (of the healing scripture types) do you relate to the most? Why?

3 DELIVERANCE

Deliverance can come quickly and quietly through prayer or revelation from Christ. It can also come in other ways. The minister must know that should there be a demonic stronghold in a person, there may be resistance to eviction.

A demon can not possess a person unless there is some bondage in that person. A demon must go out as there is prayer for a person's liberty from sin or bad habits or addictions.

Matthew 10: [7] And as ye go, preach, saying, The kingdom of heaven is at hand.

[8] Heal the sick, cleanse the lepers, raise the dead, cast out devils: freely ye have received, freely give.

I've been a part of praying for people to be healed when a demon manifested in the person. The person no longer resembles himself or herself. The person does not sound the same or act the same. The person can be thrown to the ground and shaken. The minister must remain in Christ's authority and command the demon to release the person. Christians cast our demons by the authority of Jesus blood. This ministry of deliverance is essential. The ministry team must know that nothing, no one can resist the blood of Jesus, the name of Jesus, the authority of Jesus. Should an occurrence arise, the altar worker should know to call for a senior minister. There should always be pastors, elders and deacons at the altar.

Prayer of faith shall save the sick

James 5: [13] Is any among you afflicted? let him pray. Is any merry? let him sing psalms.
[14] Is any sick among you? let him call for the elders of the church; and let them pray over him, anointing him with oil in the name of the Lord:

[15] And the prayer of faith shall save the sick, and the Lord shall raise him up; and if he have committed sins, they shall be forgiven him.

[16] Confess your faults one to another, and pray one for another, that ye may be healed. The effectual fervent prayer of a righteous man availeth much.

The person can be healed in spirit, soul and body.

Forgiveness

Matthew 6: [14] For if ye forgive men their trespasses, your heavenly Father will also forgive you:
[15] But if ye forgive not men their trespasses, neither will your Father forgive your trespasses.

It is necessary that Christians immediately forgive anyone who has offended them. If you do not forgive, you can not be forgiven. Jesus requires us to hold no grudge or ill will towards anyone. Many people hold onto something that was done against them and it festers like an infection in a wound. It distorts the person, it cause the person to think bad thoughts against someone. It is necessary to receive the blood of Jesus and to apply the blood of Jesus by faith – to any hurt or wound. People can do it unintentionally. They are easy for our human selves to forgive.

There are people who hurt others intentionally. It is against human nature to forgive them. It is only the blood of Jesus that can do it. You may not feel like forgiving; you may not want to forgive – after all you shouldn't be treated that way – but our example of forgiveness does not come from human logic or human explanation. Jesus is our example. As he was dying on the cross, he spoke

" Forgive them for they know not what they do." (Luke 23: 34) Jesus in agony – obeyed the Spirit of God within Him. He did not blame anyone.

Jesus is our example. Although we may not have the strength or will to forgive someone, we must. Say out loud – I forgive so and so… by the blood of Jesus. I apply the blood of Jesus to this area. I thank you Jesus that I no longer hold anything against that person. I receive the blood of Jesus cleansing that person – freeing that person. I receive the blood of Jesus in my life – covering that situation. It's necessary once. But if any ill will towards that person returns – stand strong. Say it once more. Keep saying it. You can also start praying blessings on that person. Choose scriptures of blessing. If the person is not a Christian – pray for his or her salvation. If the person is a Christian pray for prosperity, peace, abundance, strong relationships, health etc. Start praying for someone that way and you will start loving the person. Nothing is more powerful that the blood of Jesus. Forgiveness starts with obedience to Scripture.

As ministers at the altar – should a person request healing with anointing with oil, it is necessary the people be trained to ask the person if there is unforgiveness. If there is, state it – you must forgive so you can receive forgiveness. Often people who receive anointing with oil are healed as they forgive should that have been a factor. The oil is not magical, or mystical - nor does it serve no purpose. It is representative of the Holy Spirit and the healing power of God. Application of the oil in faith – is a sacrament. It should be a regular part of our ministry at the altar.

Chapter questions
1. You were set free by the blood of Jesus Christ. Explain what changed in your life.
2. Did you the deliverance of someone? Describe it.
3. Did you minister deliverance to anyone? Describe it.

4 MARRIAGE

The altar is a place of offering. It was established by Moses as a place for the offering of animals. The altar is essential in Christian Marriage because the man, the woman are making a covenant with each other as well as with God in the presence of Christian witnesses. The ceremony occurs at the altar or on the platform – depending on the Church; nevertheless it is a sacrament – a holy ceremony at the altar. The marriage ceremony is meant to be a lifelong commitment to each other with God. The following chapter discusses the importance of marriage as a sacrament. The relationship is with God's presence and with God as a part of the commitment. The vows are not only with each other but with God. The ministry team in a wedding is the senior pastor or one of the pastors. The congregation agree in prayer. The ceremony is at the altar because it is a covenant with God.

Marriage Sacrament   (from my book on The Sacraments: a Charismatic Guide. (2017, Living Word)

Marriage is a sacrament. It is more than an agreement. It is also a covenant that people make with each other and with God. There is an action or obedience part that we do but it has spiritual significance. God hates divorce. Marriage is the ceremony of making vows or promises to a person and to God to keep these vows throughout both their lives. Although permission for divorce was given to Moses to give to Israel, it is not God's best choice for people.

Matthew 19 [4] And he answered and said unto them, Have ye not read, that he which made them at the beginning made them male and female,

[5] And said, For this cause shall a man leave father and mother, and shall cleave to his wife: and they twain shall be one flesh?

Matthew 19: 8 He said to them, "Moses, for the hardness of your hearts, permitted you to divorce your wives, but from the beginning it was not so. 9 But I say to you, whoever divorces his wife, except for sexual immorality, and marries another, commits adultery. And whoever marries her who is divorced commits adultery."

Covenant Aspect of Marriage

Often people do not want to make such serious commitments so they simply live together or have prenuptial agreements. These agreements are based on what should happen should they divorce. Such agreements imply that the people will stay together only as long as they both want it that way. The covenant aspect of marriage almost is never emphasized. In the book of God of Covenant: God's relationship with Man, I describe in more detail the making of a covenant with someone. It usually meant the shedding of blood of both parties making the covenant. Each person vows to care for the other until death. It is more serious than a treaty or promise. It is promised with the life blood of each person, who are in agreement that should the other person need assistance or help, the other will come to defend him or die trying to.

Marriage is mentioned by God referring to Adam and Eve. Eve was created as a companion for Adam, so he wouldn't be alone. They were created as equals. There are so many excellent teachings I could recommend to you. For instance, Eve was created from Adam's rib – from his side, meaning she was not beneath him or above him. They were equal. Adam would have someone to love and speak with and they were commanded to multiply. God wanted them to have as many children as possible. Sex was God's idea. It is meant to be pleasurable. God wanted people to fill all the earth.

Genesis 2: 24 Therefore a man will leave his father and his mother and be joined to his wife, and they will become one flesh.

After the flood, Noah and his family are given the same commandment to replenish the earth by multiplying. God wanted there to be many people on earth. Marriage was the ordained way of two people joining together to live as one family.

Matthew 19: 4 He answered, "Have you not read that He who made them at the beginning 'made them male and female,'[a] 5 and said, 'For this reason a man shall leave his father and mother and be joined to his wife, and the two shall become one flesh'[b]? 6 So they are no longer two, but one flesh. Therefore, what God has joined together, let no man put asunder."

The Joining

The words used indicate a coming together of lives. They both agree their lives will be lived together. A person should not lightly enter into such an agreement with any person let alone God Himself. In Christian marriage, God is welcomed and present in the ceremony. The two people are not only making their vows to one another but also to and with God. Such a commitment is sacred. It is the joining of two lives for the glory of God with God as the witness. It literally means they ask God to be in the midst of the marriage. It means both the man and the woman respect God as the leader of the home. They agree to live according to God's Word and to honour each other with their words, actions and lives for all of their lives. God as the head of the home means the Word of God is honored above feelings or disagreements. Both of them, agree to keep God as the center of their marriage.

Ecclesiastes 4: A threefold cord is not quickly broken.

Two people can go to almost any place to arrange for a marriage certificate, without a ceremony and without inviting God into the midst of the marriage. They can focus on their verbal agreement with each other and ignore God or leave God out of it. The relationship is without the presence of God. Two people who make an agreement together can give their best. The man could give 100%. The woman could give 100%. Some days though, perhaps the man can only give 60% towards the marriage because of circumstances. The woman would have to give herself 100% but there would still not be harmony in the home. She would be living giving and giving, all one sided. The same is also true concerning the woman. Perhaps, she could only give 70% effort towards their marriage. The man could give 100% but it wouldn't be enough for their relationship.

If God is in the marriage, God always gives 100%. God never gives less. Sometimes, He gives more. He can strengthen the man or the woman supernaturally so that the marriage is smooth no matter what should occur. God's presence both in their hearts and at the center of their marriage ensures that they are built up, encouraged and strengthened. God should be the head of the relationship and the head of the home.

Living Together without Marriage

Some people believe they want to "try" the relationship and live together before they get married. It feels like a marriage almost. The truth is they have not made a true commitment. If you want to live with someone and have intimate relations with that person, you should marry. If you once knew God, and are living with someone, you should marry – even if it is only getting that people of paper. It becomes official in your country and you have made a serious commitment.

I know that weddings can be expensive, especially should you have a church wedding with dinner. The point is you could do it economically if you spoke with a pastor and got the congregation to help you. I have known several young couples who had been living together but came back to our church to marry and to rededicate their lives to God because they wanted their children to be Christians. Our church would usually host a party for them. People would bring desserts and salads and there would be someone volunteer to cook meat. It was not as fancy as a big hall with a live band, but it was a church family that was forgiving and accepting, welcoming them to return. It is important that it be done publicly. You can invite your friends and family to witness the marriage. This is the best possible choice. It shows a sincere desire to make God the center of the home. It should be in a church that you go to.

There are people who will get married in a church and pay for the service but never attend the church. They rent the hall; they rent the preacher. They do not make a commitment to the church. I have known of other people, who are not living for God but believe it is important to get married in a church.

Prerequisites for Marriage

Many churches offer Bible classes before marriage. Some make it mandatory. I believe it is an excellent way of giving the people teaching on the Biblical view of marriage. I also believe it should be essential that the people know their life's callings and their spiritual giftings before they marry. Often the couple have complimentary gifts. For instance, he may be a servant and she may be a teacher. Together they are a mighty witness for God. There should be spiritual instruction given to the couple as well as practical Biblical teaching.

Marriage is a most serious commitment. In the Old Testament, a man could not be called into the army if he recently married. He had to stay at home for one year before he could enlist. A man could not make other commitments within that first year of marriage.

Deuteronomy 24: 5 When a man has taken a new wife, he shall not go out to war or be charged with any business; he is to be free at home one year, and must bring joy to his wife which he has taken.

The New Testament mentioning of marriage does not change from God's original speaking to Moses. The husbands and wives are to respect and honour each other in their relationship with God and with each other. Jesus is the example given. Just as Christ the head and Saviour of the Church, suffered and died to redeem His bride, the Church, so should a man love his wife. The husband should be willing to lay down his life to protect and care for his wife. The wife should submit to her husband. I know the word 'submit' releases all kinds of groanings in both women and men. As a single person, you submit to God and your parents. Submit is not a negative word. It means you agree with them.

Ephesians 5: 22 Wives, be submissive to your own husbands as unto the Lord. 23 For the husband is the head of the wife, just as Christ is the head and Savior of the church, which is His body. 24 But as the church submits to Christ, so also let the wives be to their own husbands in everything.

A person is never to submit to ungodly treatment by his or her spouse. A person is not to submit to abuse of any kind. A person is not to submit to anything less than Jesus' example of someone who lays down his life to care for his spouse. Jesus ransomed His Bride, the Church, through His love that compelled him to suffer, die and rise from the dead so we could be free from sin and its curse. Jesus is returning to earth one day soon; He is coming as a Bridegroom for His Bride, the Church. God compares the most sacred relationship we have with our Saviour and the hope of His return to a marriage. That means God considers marriage to be sacred. In both living for Jesus Christ and living in a marriage, the two become one. We are to become one with God for all of eternity.

Marriage is spiritual

If you are married to the right person, God will speak to that person concerning you. If you do not know it is the right person, you should never marry that person. God can give words of wisdom, words of knowledge and words of prophecy concerning your life to your spouse. That is not only one way. I know many women who God has spoken to and given spiritual wisdom to speak to their husbands because God sees the marriage as one family unit. The husband is to love his wife as he loves himself. That means he will do everything possible to give the best and the choicest to his wife. He would care about her desires as well as her gifts.

Ephesians 5: 25 Husbands, love your wives, just as Christ also loved the church and gave Himself for it, 26 that He might sanctify and cleanse it with the washing of water by the word, 27 and that He might present to Himself a glorious church, not having spot, or wrinkle, or any such thing, but that it should be holy and without blemish. 28 In this way men ought to love their wives as their own bodies. He who loves his wife loves himself. 29 For no one ever hated his own flesh, but nourishes and cherishes it, just as the Lord cares for the church. 30 For we are members of His body, of His flesh and of His bones. 31 "For this reason a man shall leave his father and mother and shall be joined to his wife, and the two shall be one flesh."[a] 32 This is a great mystery, but I am speaking about Christ and the church. 33 However, let each one of you love his wife as himself, and let the wife see that she respects her husband.

Love for your wife

One of the best descriptions of a husband's love for his wife that I have heard is Mahesh Chavda speak about God dealing very seriously with him about not only letting his wife explore her gifts and talents but encouraging her to use her gifts and talents. He wept as he said God showed him how much God loved her and her spiritual growth was a top priority. He caused him to change in how he saw her. He should pray for her not only with her. She should pray for him and with him. In this way, they will be honouring God and each other.

The man and the woman should encourage and strengthen each other. In this scripture both the husband and wife are commanded to submit to each other. There is equality in their relationship. There is the promise that neither the husband nor the wife would treat the other less than his or herself. A wise woman knows her husband cares for her spiritually and she should listen to what he is speaking to her. A wise husband knows that his wife has special insight and care for him like no other person on earth. They are made to complement each other as a whole.

Ephesians 5: 20 Give thanks always for all things to God the Father in the name of our Lord Jesus Christ, 21 being submissive to one another in the fear of God.

You are Complete in Christ

I want to come against the lie that the woman completes the man or the man completes the woman. You are not a half. If you are only half a person, you do not know Jesus Christ. If you get married so someone will complete you, you will never be happy. No person on earth can complete you. Only God can fill you so you are complete. God living in us completes us.

Colossians 2: 9 For in Him lives all the fullness of the Godhead bodily. 10 And you are complete in Him, who is the head of all authority and power.

You should marry because you believe God has brought that person into your life and that you would be complimentary to each other, helping each other and strengthening each other. You should marry because you believe that person would be a good parent to your children. You should know without a doubt the person respects and honours and cherishes you. Certainly, there will be physical attraction; there will be spiritual attraction etc. Husbands and wives should build each other up spiritually. They should speak and pray scripture over each other.

Ephesians 5: 26 that He might sanctify and cleanse it with the washing of water by the word, 27 and that He might present to Himself a glorious church, not having spot, or wrinkle, or any such thing, but that it should be holy and without blemish. 28 In this way men ought to love their wives as their own bodies. He who loves his wife loves himself

Your relationship should be spiritual in that you encourage each other to be the best possible. This would include praying for each other's gifts and talents and success as though you were praying for yourself. Normally the wife gets special intuition about things, and if she is a godly woman, she is praying about them and speaking to her husband about them.

Made One

The husband is to love God first and his wife next. The same is true of the wife. God must be first and her husband next. If they truly keep these as the priorities, their relationship will go smoothly. I knew of a pastor who would not let people get divorced until they met with her. She would get them both to come together and she moved mightily in the gift of prophecy and word of wisdom and word of knowledge. She would often pray with them, and before the end of the meeting they would both be repenting for their neglect or abuse of the other. They got right with God; they got right with each other. This would be the best way for our churches to function. Not all pastors have those same prophetic giftings,

I know of a couple who were married more than 30 years who loved each other and had a glow of joy about them. They loved each other and they both were servants in the church. They shared with me one of the best resolutions to arguments that I've ever known. They both agreed together they would never let the sun go down without making up with each other. What they would do, is get a basin of warm water and a towel and even if they were mad at each other, they would pray for the other person and wash the person's feet.

As you are kneeling there at your spouse's feet loving the person as Christ loved his disciples, as you pray blessings over the person and scriptures, God will empty you of any self-righteousness or pride. People who do this – put Christ first, no matter how they are feeling, are sure to stay together. They both agree that Christ is first. I would also recommend taking communion with your spouse and recommitting yourselves to each other with prayer. A man and woman who are in union with God are unstoppable. They can do much for Christ's kingdom together. They must be in agreement. You cannot yoke a donkey and an ox because both walk differently. They must both walk the same. Your point of agreement in your marriage should always be that God is the center.

Don't Eliminate Christ from your Marriage

Don't forget that God is the center of your personal life and your marriage. Don't let anything replace your conversations with your spouse. Television should never be the focus of the family. It is for entertainment; it should never take priority over your spouse. Don't let your cell phone be your priority. Don't put anything above your relationship with God or with your spouse. It doesn't mean the other things can't be a part of what you do but they should never define you.

The reason the Apostle Paul states that some people should remain single as himself is because the husband must care for his wife. The wife must care for her husband. It is a commandment that God gives. A married person can't do anything he or she wants without speaking to his or her spouse and discussing it. You become not only accountable to God but also to each other.

You and your spouse should be praying together every day. I understand that children and pets and working spouses etc. add some complexity but there should be moments of sincere prayer for each other each day.

I have known couples who have been married, 30, 40, 50 years or longer, who lived faithfully loving each other keeping God first. I have known others who lived through terrible things such as unfaithfulness of a spouse but they were reconciled and their marriage was restored. With God in your marriage, you will never lose. Should a couple shut God out of their marriage, most certainly they will not love each other with the unconditional love I have mentioned. They could end in divorce. There are excellent books on marriage by Myles Munroe. I highly recommend them. They give a Christ centered teaching on marriage and how to truly love your spouse.

Your inviting of God into the marriage ceremony is not only as a witness that one day you got married. It is for God to be the head of your marriage relationship all the days of your life. This is the sacrament aspect that is spiritual. God is dwelling in both of you and also in your covenant made to each other with God.

If you Wonder if You're Ready, you are not

Do not marry too quickly. The ideal is that you both would have done some Bible study together and talked about spiritual things as well as natural things. You would know the other person's likes and dislikes. You may know the other person's weaknesses and strengths. Examine all these things before you get married; don't marry so you can change the other person. You should be able to share with your potential spouse as with the closest friend the desires of your heart knowing that he or she will care and pray about them and want the best possible for you also. Just as God wants to give you the desires of your heart, your spouse should want you to be joyful and successful.

Psalm 37: 4 4 Delight yourself in the Lord,
   and He will give you the desires of your heart.

A Recommendation for Those who Want to Marry

Many people get married in the Romance stage of the marriage. This means the other person seems perfect and the attraction is so strong he or she doesn't notice the habits of the person or the person's demeanor or the person's mannerisms. Usually, I would recommend the couple wait at least a year. It is not stated as such in scripture; I only speak by personal experience and many people I have known who married and are successful and also some who are not. I also believe they should be doing spiritual studying together as well as prayer and serving, The more they use their spiritual giftings together, the smoother they will see how to complement each other. Get to know the person's behaviour before you marry.

1 Corinthians 7: 9 But if they cannot restrain themselves, let them marry. For it is better to marry than to burn with passion.

Adultery and Fornication

Exodus 20: 14 You shall not commit adultery.

The commandment is for singles as well as married people. There is to be no sex outside of marriage. The commandment is clear but in our society it is not honoured. There are even Christians who are engaged to be married who are tempted and have sexual relations outside of marriage: fornication. They may believe it is okay because they plan to marry eventually. It is sin. I heard of Kenneth Copeland talk about this matter and it was excellent. He said that you should both repent. Get with your fiancée and both of you confess it to God and plead the blood over yourselves and commit to God that from that moment on you will remain pure before marriage. Kenneth Copeland said to take communion with one another and vow to live holy so that God will bless you and bless your marriage. If we truly repent, God forgives us and empowers us so that we do not have to live in sin.

Spiritual Aspects of Marriage

The two people are joining their lives and they will likely have children. Most people marry for that purpose; it is not the only reason to marry but Biblically, God did command them to be fruitful and multiply. God never revoked His word. Should you have children, you both need wisdom from God. To nurture and encourage the children as well as teach them spiritual and natural things, requires spiritual discernment and divine leading. Marriage is a most serious, solemn covenant that should not be considered lightly. If you commit adultery in your marriage, you are not only breaking your covenant with your spouse but also with God. Neglecting your spouse, or drawing apart from him or her is also a sin. Some people say they grew apart. That should be impossible because marriage is the two becoming one. That means there must be communion, a sharing of lives, not simply sexual relations. If you do not want to live together as one, you should not be getting married.

1 Corinthians 7: 5 Do not deprive one another except with consent for a time, that you may give yourselves to fasting and prayer. Then come together again, so that Satan does not tempt you for lack of self-control.

Marriage means a joining together until the death of the spouse except by mutual agreement. If you are not sure you are ready to join your life to someone, don't marry. God's standard for marriage is high; it is a lifelong commitment. You should consider the person you marry carefully. You should learn each other's character traits before you marry. Our churches should preach commitment for life marriage. God can give you special love for your spouse. God can correct your spouse. I don't know if you have seen the movie War Room that came out in 2016, but it was an excellent movie about prayer and how God can save a marriage if one of the partners is praying. I knew of a miraculous restoration of a marriage.

The man and woman were Christians. As their marriage became seasoned, he cheated (had relationships with other women) on her more and more. He ended the marriage relationship by leaving the woman and moving in with his girlfriend. He completely turned away from God as well as his spouse. They became divorced. It was not her decision but it happened. That woman was a prayer warrior. She prayed over her husband – she never broke her part of the covenant with God.

She was an attractive woman with money. She could have found a different person. She chose to pray for him. She would pray for him to repent and for the resurrection of her marriage based on God's covenant with the both of them. She did this day after day, year after year. She still loved him. He did not treat her well if they saw each other, it only bothered her more so she moved to a different state, but she continued the praying and would make visits home to see her family and hear about her ex-husband. For twenty years, she prayed and travailed and kept the prayer faithfully for his repentance and the resurrection of their marriage.

I do not know of anyone else who had the vision so clear for her marriage to be restored. Perhaps people might have thought she was extreme because she did not give up on him. One day, it happened. It came as a surprise to all of us who knew about her situation but not to her. She shouted and danced and praised God with all her being. He repented. He begged her to come back. He rededicated his life to God. They remarried. Twenty years of constant believing and praying, she saw the desire of her heart. She believed God would do it. God would never violate a human will. Even though he made terrible choices and abandoned her and turned away from God, God let him. She completely had grace to forgive him.

Divorced

There is mercy for people who have sinned. There is one acceptable reason for divorce and remarriage. It is not God's perfect plan but He allows it. If one of the person's is unfaithful, divorce is permitted. They can remarry freely.

Matthew 19: 8 He said to them, "Moses, for the hardness of your hearts, permitted you to divorce your wives, but from the beginning it was not so. 9 But I say to you, whoever divorces his wife, except for sexual immorality, and marries another, commits adultery. And whoever marries her who is divorced commits adultery."

There are a multitude of reasons for divorce. Abuse, neglect, character traits, habits etc. Please know that I know the divorce rate is high. There is mercy for those who sin. I'm saying with boldness God can forgive you for any sin. Go to Jesus; even if it is not your doing, pray submitting yourself wholly to God and giving yourself to God. I have known of people who God shines light on and their lives are resurrected. Divorce is so tough one people because first, it is a covenant with the partner and with God. Only God can heal someone who has suffered from divorce. The good news is that God can and does heal.

Christian Parents

A Christian mother should in all matters teach the children the things of God. Usually, but not always does the mother spend more time with the children than their dad does. She should read with them, pray with them as well as help them in all natural matters. So should he care for them. I have known of single moms and single dads who invest all their efforts into the raising of the children. I have seen these single parents training their children in the best way possible even though they are working, paying bills, speaking with an uncooperative spouse etc. It is really God's mercy over them. Christian parents are a covering for their children until their children are old enough to accept Jesus themselves.

Deuteronomy 11: 19 You shall teach them to your children, speaking of them when you sit in your house and when you walk by the way, when you lie down, and when you rise up.

Both the husband and the wife should have separate prayer as well as prayer together. I have known of Christian husbands who would arise and go to 6am prayer services before work. They knew God had entrusted his family to him. He knew that only with God could he get wisdom and discernment and knowledge to lead and cover in prayer as a shield of protection over his family. I have known of Christian women who would rise early to begin praying before the school day. They would pray evenings and throughout the day. I mean they would pray about their children and family members as well as others. They literally were living the apostle Paul's commandment to "Pray without ceasing." 1 Thessalonians 5: 17.

Christian Family Anointing

Christian marriage partners should be growing spiritually together as well as individually. This type of bonding usually comes through sharing Christian service such as evangelism or praise teams or serving together during church functions. I have been privileged to know a Christian family of worshippers. As they lead worship, they flowed together so smoothly and completely in the Holy Spirit. The family radiated the love of God as they worshipped. It was a special family anointing on them as they worshipped together. They all have individual talents and ministry giftings but as a family, a unique dynamic occurs as the Holy Spirit fills them and flows through them.

I believe every Christian couple has a ministry anointing. I believe that every Christian family has an anointing for service. They should pray and seek God about what they are to do as a family. I believe God will speak to both the husband and the wife. I believe that God will confirm the word. The family will find joy in serving the LORD together. I have seen families volunteer to serve at banquets or who cook together, or who minister together, preaching and teaching God. I believe that the Husband and the wife should pray for a vision of what God would have them to do as a family. It is a spiritual union with God in the midst of it. God wants to use you as a family to impact the earth for God.

Renewing vows – marriage can be for spiritual reasons – some use it as a celebration Rejoice in the wife of your youth Prov 15: 18 Ecc 9:9 Solomon 4:12

Chapter Questions

1. Did you get married with a covenant understanding of marriage? Describe it.
2. If you did not – but believe it is important, consider praying with your spouse a renewal of vows. Some may way to proclaim them publicly at your church.
3. Examine your marriage situation – are you giving your 100% in the marriage? Is your partner? Is there always Christ in your marriage. Consider it. Discuss it with your spouse. Pray together concerning it.
4. If you are not yet married – pray over yourself the fruit of the Spirit – that Christ would transform your innermost being. Pray for a godly spouse with the qualities described in Ephesians 5. Do not accept less than someone who would love you as Christ loves the Church.

5 DEDICATION OF CHILDREN

The dedication of children occurs at the altar because it is a lifelong vow of parents, pastors, elders and the congregation to raise the child in a Christian atmosphere with Christian truths. The ministry team includes the pastors, elders, deacons, parents. The congregation prays with them as each child is prayed over.

The Dedication of Children – Sacrament

Christians offer their children to God and vow to raise them as Christians in the sacrament of baby dedication. It occurs at the altar – the place of offering. In the Churches of my life, the pastors as well as deacons and elders surround the parents and their child (children) and pray over them. The following excerpt is from my book on the Sacraments: A Charismatic Guide.

In most Protestant Churches, this sacrament is practiced. In some denominations, the children are Christened – meaning they are baptized but not immersed in the water – sprinkled with water. It is really a way of the parents agreeing to raise their children as Christians. The Bible teaches believer's baptism, that is total immersion over someone proclaiming to believe that Jesus Christ died for all sinners, rose from the dead and ascended into heaven and is coming again. Children who are infants who do not know the LORD Jesus Christ as their personal Saviour and LORD should be dedicated by the parents. It is a way of honouring the LORD. It is a way of presenting the child to God, in agreement with the Word of God that instructs parents to teach their children the Word of God. It means the parents are living as Christians and will instruct their children in the ways of God.

Usually, dedication of children is scheduled as part of the church service. The parents dress the children in the cutest outfits and they stand with the pastor and sometimes the elders who will pray blessings over the child. A scripture may be read or prayed over the child. The parents are standing before the congregation to pledge they will raise their children as Christians. The congregation is praying that the child will come to know Christ at an early age. The pastor usually consecrates the child by praying that God would bless and keep the child.

In some churches, prayer is made that the parents will be faithful in the raising of their children to serve God. Although prayer for the parents is good, the dedication of children should be about praying over the children. The fact that the parents are coming in front of the church with their child or children, is usually a testimony of them wanting to raise the child as a Christian.

At some baby dedications, there is prophesy over the children. Usually it is the pastor or the ministry team who pray prophetically over the children, as the Holy Spirit leads. What that means is, the Holy Spirit is the author of the prophecy. God gives the person the unction, the words and the anointing to pray prophetically over the children.

Not a Ritual

We do not simply carry our children in front of the church so that people can see them and how cute they are. It is not simply an outward action. If there is no faith, there is nothing that happens. The parents must believe that dedicating their children is a consecration of the children and the hope for a blessing to be imparted by the prayers of the ministers and the local body of Christ. I'm saying we believe the children are separated unto God and "covered" by the faith of the parents.

1 Corinthians 7: 14 For the unbelieving husband is sanctified by the wife, and the unbelieving wife is sanctified by the husband. Otherwise, your children would be unclean. But now they are holy.

Sacrament

There are two parts because it is a sacrament. There is a natural presentation of the children in front of the pastors and congregation and there is a spiritual proclamation of consecration of the children to God. It is a way of honouring what Jesus did by laying hands on children and praying a blessing over them.

Matthew 19: 13 Then little children were brought to Him that He might put His hands on them and pray. But the disciples rebuked them.

14 But Jesus said, "Let the little children come to Me, and do not forbid them. For to such belongs the kingdom of heaven." 15 He laid His hands on them and departed from there.

Jesus Shows Priorities

Jesus corrected his disciples who perhaps believed the children were not important. Jesus called for the children and prayed blessings over them. I do not believe Jesus was doing a ritual. I am sure Jesus was truly imparting a blessing. It was Jesus, the Messiah, God himself in human form. He was praying blessings on the children. He was praying the best possible life for those children. Jesus wants the best for us. If He believed it was important to bless the children, we also should see the significance.

Luke 18: 15 They also brought infants to Him that He might touch them. When the disciples saw it, they rebuked them. 16 But Jesus called them to Him and said, "Permit the little children to come to Me, and do not hinder them. For to such belongs the kingdom of God. 17 Truly, I say to you, whoever will not receive the kingdom of God as a little child will in no wise enter it."

Jesus used the children to preach to the people. He preached that all must receive the kingdom of God as innocently and with pure motives as children would press into someone they loved. It is normal for a child or children to cling to their parents especially in a new environment. We also should press into Jesus. We should know He wants only the best for us as a parent would shelter a child.

Jesus' Dedication as a Child

Luke 2: 21 When eight days had passed and the Child was circumcised, He was named JESUS, the name given by the angel before He was conceived in the womb.

22 When the days of her purification according to the Law of Moses were completed, they brought Him to Jerusalem to present Him to the Lord 23 (as it is written in the law of the Lord, "Every firstborn male shall be called holy to the Lord"[a]) 24 and to offer a sacrifice according to what is said in the law of the Lord, "a pair of turtledoves, or two young pigeons."[b]

Prophetic Prayer

Jesus himself was presented for circumcision and to offer a sacrifice thanking God for the child. Mary and Joseph honoured the LORD in obeying the Mosaic covenant. Simeon a prophet of God who prayed constantly that he could live to see the Messiah that would come to redeem Israel was present in the temple and was moved by the Holy Spirit to prophesy over Jesus.

Luke 2: 29 "Lord, now let Your servant depart in peace,

according to Your word;
30 for my eyes have seen Your salvation
31   which You have prepared in the sight of all people,
32 a light for revelation to the Gentiles,   and the glory of Your people Israel."

Simeon also prophesied over Mary. He gave words that she would hold on to throughout the life and death of Jesus.

Luke 2: Listen, this Child is destined to cause the fall and rising of many in Israel and to be a sign which will be spoken against, 35 so that the thoughts of many hearts may be revealed. And a sword will pierce through your own soul also."

Also, in the temple praying was Anna, a godly woman who gave her life to prayer and fasting after her husband died. She also was moved by the Holy Spirit to prophesy over the infant Jesus.

Luke 2: 36 And there was Anna a prophetess, a daughter of Phanuel, of the tribe of Asher. She was of a great age and had lived with her husband seven years from her virginity. 37 And she was a widow of about eighty-four years of age who did not depart from the temple, but served God with fasting and prayer night and day. 38 Coming at that moment she gave thanks to the Lord and spoke of Him to all those who looked for the redemption of Jerusalem.

The Prophesying is Important

The prophecies over the children are important. It was important for Jesus. Those two individuals did not know the miraculous birth of Jesus or his destiny except through the Holy Spirit. Any special prayers or prophesy over the children should be recorded so that they could be used for prayer and for guidance for the parents and those who raise the child. Some prophesies may come over a child. It may or may not occur depending on may factors. Some ministers do not flow in the prophetic so they wouldn't be moved to prophesy. Some churches are on strict schedules so they may not wait for the promptings of the Spirit for the prophetic. It doesn't necessarily automatically come for each child. If there were a gathering of Apostles and prophets praying over the children, I would expect there to be prophesy over the children. Not everyone flows in these giftings or in these expectations from the LORD.

The Dedication of the Child

The dedication of a child is an announcement in the faith of God for their child or children to become Christians. They are literally giving the best offering they could give to God – that child or those children. The parents are promising to obey God. The minister consecrates the child. The congregation prays for the child.

The Mosaic Covenant

According to the Mosaic covenant, all of the first born of all creatures were to be given to God. The first-born animals, were given as a sacrifice. The children were redeemed by giving an offering. It was a way of remembering the miracles God did to set Israel free from Egyptian bondage – especially the Passover celebration. It was a way of thanking God and giving the best offering possible to thank God for the child.

Exodus 22: 29 You must not delay to offer the first of your harvest and of your vats.

You must give to Me the firstborn of your sons. 30 Likewise you must do the same with your oxen and with your sheep. Seven days it shall remain with its mother, but on the eighth day you must give it to Me.

Exodus 13: 13 But every first offspring of a donkey you shall redeem with a lamb. And if you do not redeem it, then you shall break its neck, and all the firstborn of man among your sons you shall redeem. 14 "It shall be when your son asks you in time to come, saying, 'What is this?' that you shall say to him, 'With a strong hand the Lord brought us out from Egypt, from the house of bondage. 15 And when Pharaoh stubbornly refused to let us go, that the Lord killed all the firstborn in the land of Egypt, both the firstborn of man, and the firstborn of beast. Therefore, I sacrifice to the Lord the first male offspring of every womb, but all the firstborn of my sons I redeem.' 16 It shall be as a sign on your hand and as frontlets on your forehead, for with a strong hand the Lord brought us out of Egypt."

Hanna prays for a child

Hanna in the Old testament book of Samuel wanted a child so much she prayed and fasted in the temple until one day the priest blessed her by saying may the Lord grant you your request. She made a vow to God that if God would open her womb so that she may have a child, she would give him to God for service. Within a year of that priest's words of blessing and much praying by Hanna, she gave birth to a son and named him Samuel.

1 Samuel 1: 21 Then the man Elkanah and all his house went up to offer to

the Lord the yearly sacrifice and his vow. 22 But Hannah did not go, for she said to her husband, "I will not go up until the child is weaned, and then I will bring him, that he may appear before the Lord and live there forever."

She cared for the child and after he was weaned, she presented him at the Temple to the priest as she had promised God she would do. She brought Samuel and an offering to God thanking God for the child and to consecrate the child to the service of God. She presented the best that she had to God – the child she had prayed for. The child Samuel was raised by the priest. He was trained to serve the LORD. Each year Hanna brought clothing for her son. God blessed her with other children because she kept her vow. A vow to God is very important.

1 Samuel 1: 24 When she had weaned him, she took him up with her with three bulls, one ephah[b] of flour, and a bottle of wine. And she brought him to the house of the Lord in Shiloh, though the boy was young. 25 Then they slaughtered a bull, and they brought the boy to Eli. 26 And she said, "Oh, my lord! As you live, my lord, I am the woman that stood by you here praying to the Lord. 27 For this boy I prayed, and the Lord has given me my petition which I asked of Him. 28 Therefore also I have let the Lord have him. As long as he lives he will be dedicated to the Lord." And he worshipped the Lord there.

Children are a gift from God

One of the main commandments God gave to Adam and Eve and later Noah is to have as many children as possible. God commanded that they be fruitful and multiply. Children were treasured by their parents. Not only would they help with the family business once they were older, they would carry on the family name. They would pass on the truths they had learned about God to their children. Through this there would be a godly people on earth who worshipped Jehovah.

Psalm 127: 3 Look, children are a gift of the Lord,
    and the fruit of the womb is a reward.
4 As arrows in the hand of a mighty warrior,
    so are the children of one's youth.
5 Happy is the man
    who has his quiver full of them;
he shall not be ashamed
    when he speaks with the enemies at the gate.

Children are precious and we can teach our children to love, honour and live for God. It should come from the parents, the church and the school agreeing together in raising the children to become Christians. God entrusts to us a living soul. God gives us special responsibility and special joys in seeing the kids raised to honour God. Parents, teachers and people in the lives of children should nurture the gifts and talents in the children. We should teach them and encourage them in all spiritual truths as well as in their natural abilities.

Proverbs 22: 6 Train up a child in the way he should go,
   and when he is old he will not depart from it.

The parents who treasure their children and that serve God wholly will be gifted by God to have good relationship with their children and also be able to see the "way" for each child. This means each child is an individual and has special gifts and talents to be nurtured and encouraged. Teachers who love their students will be able to see the special expressions of talent in each child. Together parents, teachers and the local church members can contribute to the children by giving them the best possible care.

The Potential of a Child

God may entrust to our care one who will become a world evangelist, or a professor or an inventor or a doctor. Each child encouraged in his or her talents can explore gifts and talents and develop them so they are used for God's glory. A child is a gift from God. The child has some of the characteristics of each parent. The child is also unique. I have not met a Christian parent who does not believe the child is a gift from God. As the child grows, individual traits and giftings become more prominent and the child's character is formed and his or her interests can be encouraged. For example, the children can take music lessons so they can play an instrument; they can be taught to play sports. They can be taught in the word of God so that they can accept the LORD as children. All of these things can be developed before the children go to school.

It is the pleasure of the parent to see the giftings in the child. Teachers also can encourage the children to do their best. Often, I can see the child's particular giftings by teaching him or her and speaking with him or her individually. Parents should invest in their children. The child can learn and develop all types of talents including music, sports, reading, writing, math, science, etc. The things a child "leans towards" or enjoys will become evident in their early years. It is the responsibility of parents to help their children become the best possible people they can be. I have known of parents who sacrifice much for their children. They drive them to sporting events; music lessons; concerts; children's programs and events. They buy them books; they care for their children because their children are an expression of God's love to them. They realize God has given them a tremendous responsibility as well as a joy like no other.

Parenting

Christian parents are obligated to God as they promise to raise their children. Children who do not have parents that invest in them can raise themselves but it is not good. If the television is the main teacher of the child, the child will not learn God's ways. If a child is not encouraged in his or her talents and skills, those talents and skills go untapped and undeveloped. The children will do other things – it will depend on who does invest in the children.

For instance, a child left to himself or herself will hang out with children in the neighbourhood. That could be good or bad, depending on what those children are like. A loving neighbour can teach the children. He or she can share Christ with them. He or she can encourage and mentor them. A Sunday school teacher can care about the children. A teacher from school can make a difference. Teaching of Christ is what the parents should be doing.

Deuteronomy 11: 18 Therefore you must fix these words of mine in your heart and in your soul, and bind them as a sign on your hand, so that they may be as frontlets between your eyes. 19 You shall teach them to your children, speaking of them when you sit in your house and when you walk by the way, when you lie down, and when you rise up. 20 You shall write them on the doorposts of your house and on your gates, 21 so that your days and the days of your children may be multiplied in the land which the Lord swore to your fathers to give them, as long as the days of heaven on the earth.

The bottom line is if the parents won't raise the children, someone will, but the parents will be accountable for not doing their best with what God has entrusted to them. The responsibility of parents is to teach their children the ways of the LORD, to provide food and shelter and love. The parents should be helping the children with their homework, take interest in their schooling and their lessons. The parents should encourage the children's dreams and aspirations and be prayerful about all aspects of parenting. If the children are living in your home, they are within the sphere of your authority.

The Parents who Dedicate their Children

The parents who dedicate their children are coming into agreement with

God concerning the raising of the child. The parents are agreeing to do the best possible to train up their children.

Hands should be laid on the child to pray, to confirm gifts and talents and to completely agree on raising that child for God's best possible life.

At the church, I currently attend, the parents choose a scripture to pray over their child at dedication. I would highly encourage that those scriptures be prayerfully chosen. If the parents will join their faith to the scriptures they pray over their children, God will honour their faith.

God can give special wisdom and knowledge to Christian parents who will go with the promptings of the Holy Spirit for their children. If the parents are living in the Spirit, God will deal with them in the Spirit. If they seriously, prayerfully raise their children, God will give special insight and wisdom. God will hold us accountable for our dealings with our children because there is a spiritual responsibility that we have to model a Christian life for them and to train them up as Christians.

By the Holy Spirit

The ministers and elders should be praying a spiritual blessing over the child but also that every gift and talent will be developed, that God would draw them so that an early age the child will give his or her life to God. God can use a minister of God who will obey the promptings of the LORD to prophesy a blessing over the child. It is not simply an outward ritual. It is a faith expression and an offering to commit to raise the children to the best of their ability: the parents, the church agreeing.

As Hanna gave her son Samuel to be raised by the priest Eli, she kept her vow, so should the parents offer their children to God to be raised as unto God. As you are standing on the platform about to dedicate your child or children, God may speak to you concerning the child's life. Parents who will rely on the Holy Spirit will be guided by God in the raising of their children. God may use you in special ways to pray over your children or give you scriptures concerning your children. You should pray over your children everyday thanking God for them and praying protection and encouragement. Parenting by the Holy Spirit is God's best for your children. God can give you words of wisdom or knowledge about your children.

Sins can be passed from generation to generation. Don't let them Be. Cut them off with your generation. God can give you discerning of spirits to know if your child has inherited iniquities that must be cut off. Inherited sins can end with you as you pray over yourself and your children. If you see any type of repetitive sin in your child, you should seek God about it and deal with it in the spirit first. Cut those things off in prayer.

Numbers 14: 17 "So now, I pray, let the power of my Lord be great, just as You have spoken, saying, 18 'The Lord is slow to anger and abounding in mercy, forgiving iniquity and transgression; but He will by no means clear the guilty, visiting the iniquity of the fathers upon the children to the third and fourth generation.' 19 Pardon the iniquity of this people, I pray, according to the greatness of Your grace, just as You have pardoned this people, from Egypt even until now."

Pray in the Spirit for your children. I attended a church where we were often in long prayer meetings. You might think that the young parents wouldn't go. No. This was not the case. Parents would bring their children and a blanket. They would set their children in a place with toys or their infant in a carrier and they would attend to them – but they didn't miss prayer because of it. Their children were in an atmosphere of praise and worship and prayer often for hours. I'm not saying that the parents didn't go check on their children regularly. The fact is the children were in a atmosphere of the Holy Spirit so strong that as soon they were able to walk, they would go up to the altar and start singing and praising God themselves. No one told them to do it. The children of all ages (and adults) would sing and dance and praise God with all their being.

Search the Scriptures

Pray scriptures over your children. Most Christian bookstores carry books on the promises of God. Get a book on praying the scriptures for your children. There are books that you could get on imparting a blessing over your children. Marilyn Hickey has got an excellent book on imparting a legacy to the next generation. Pray over your children those scriptures. God may reveal something to you about the direction of your child's life. God may reveal to you to pray special protection over your child. I don't only mean while they are children. I have known of parents who pray over their children all the days of their lives. Their children are adults with children of their own, but the parents pray special blessings on their adult children. The calling to be a parent doesn't end once the child leaves home. The calling to be a parent is for all your life. long.

Please understand, I am not talking about being burdensome or smothering. Once your children marry or move out of your home, you don't have the same responsibility towards them in the natural; spiritually though, you should be praying for them. I am saying the responsibility to give your children to God only ends once your natural life ends on earth. Often the grandparents can be a strong influence. You can contribute not only to your own children's lives but also to their children's lives. This means grandparents who are being led by the Holy Spirit can make a difference in their grandchildren's lives. I know of some grandparents who were the only Christians, the parents were not living for God; those grandparents taught their grandchildren all they could about God. They invested in them scriptures, Bible stories, Sunday school etc.

Serious Prayer

I have known of Christian parents who pray for their children before the children go to school each day. Each evening, they pray a blessing over them as they tuck them in. The parents talk about God with their children and it is a normal part of their life to talk about God. The parents monitor what the children watch or listen to. The child is never left alone with only the television; these parents watch television with their children or approve of what the child sees or hears. These parents are a literal spiritual covering over the children protecting them from worldly or ungodly content.

Please, if you are a single parent, do not be insulted by any of my teaching. I understand single parents cannot invest as much as they want to into their children. I've known single moms who work two jobs to raise her children. It is tough on that parent. That is where the Christian Church should help. Offering child care in the services is very important because it gives a chance for those single parents to receive something of God. It also gives special Christian education to the children. I have been a part of some churches where the single young adults voluntarily "adopt" a child. What I mean is they will take the child to concerts or shows, play sports with the children and offer a relief to the single parent as well as a support role in the life of the child/children.

In my church, we do not have godparents. Often the term is used and any special friend is chosen. The true meaning of godparents is that if anything were to happen to the child's parents, those people would give the best possible care to the child, teaching them about the LORD. I believe it would be a wise thing to develop in all our Christian churches spiritual God Parents who would help especially single parents to raise their children as Christians. Not just anyone should be chosen. The person should be of outstanding Christian character and faith. The people should serve and honour the LORD and love you and your child. Only God can put people together in the way I am speaking about. They could be aunts and uncles or true friends. God could direct you in it. I know of no congregation such as what I am presenting, so I believe it would be up to you to seek God for wisdom about such a proposition. I believe it is essential for a child to have godly role models both men and women.

Child dedication is not always recognized in importance as it should be. God will honour you at your point of faith. Believe that God can use you to be a spiritual influence on your child. You are honouring God by presenting your child in dedication to God. You are making a covenant with God promising to raise the child and offering him or her unto God.

As one ministering in prayer for children being presented to God, we should realize the prayer has eternal significance. We should pray over the souls of the children not the cute little kids. We should pray blessings and or scriptures over the children we want to impart something of God into their lives.

Chapter questions

1. Were your children dedicated in church?
2. Did your parents dedicate you in church? Explain how you believe it affected your life.
3. Although we don't necessarily use the term godparents – are there people you would trust with your children's lives? Explain why.

6 IMPARTATION MINISTRY AR THE ALTAR

Prayer by a team of pastors, elders, deacons or apostle or prophets occurs at the front of the church is important. There may be prophecy. There may be impartation of giftings. There may be destiny decisions made there at the altar. It is almost always for special occasion such as confirmation, promotion of responsibility within the church or ordination. It is a commitment. It is the blessing of God through the ministry body towards that person or people. The following chapter from my book on the sacraments: A Charismatic Guide discusses the use in a Charismatic Church – one believing in the gifts of the Holy Spirit.

Laying on of Hands

Hebrews 6: 1 Therefore, leaving the elementary principles of the doctrine of Christ, let us go on to maturity, not laying again a foundation of repentance from dead works and of faith toward God, 2 of instruction about washings, the laying on of hands, the resurrection of the dead, and eternal judgment.

In the foundation stones of the Christian faith, laying on of hands is named as an essential foundation. It is also a sacrament. Although it is often practiced in the Christian Church in most denominations, it is not always done with faith which means it is just an external action rather than a two-part sacrament. Whatever is not of faith cannot be considered sacred. It is impossible to please God without Faith.

The Laying on of Hands

The literal Biblical interpretation is that we Christians believe that as we place hands on someone and pray for him or her, a spiritual transaction occurs. There is a transference from spirit to spirit because of the Holy Spirit and the Holy faith to do so. The Holy Spirit anointing on a person can be transferred to a believer by placing hands on the person and prayer. Faith is imparted. Sometimes, healing is imparted; sometimes confirmation of truths learned is imparted. This does not mean that prayer without laying on of hands is not effective. Jesus laid hands on people and they were healed. In some situations, in scripture, the apostles laid their hands on people for any of the above reasons.

As the disciples preached Jesus Christ after Pentecost, they had boldness to preach the infilling of the Holy Spirit or the Baptism of the Holy Spirit.

Sometimes, they simply prayed for the Spirit to come on a person, but in this instance as they shared about the Baptism of the Holy Spirit, they literally placed their hands on the believers in faith for the gift of the Holy Spirit to be given to these Samaritans.

In Acts 8: 17 Then they laid their hands on them, and they received the Holy Spirit.

Often a common method that God uses to baptism someone in the Holy Spirit is that believers filled with the Holy Spirit lay hands in faith to those who want the gift. I mean a literal transference such as this example. I throw a ball to you and you catch it in your hands. Substance is transferred. The Holy Spirit within us anoints us to lay hands for a spiritual purpose; there is a transference of spirit to spirit. The effects may not be immediate or they may be. Usually, what occurs with baptism of the Holy Spirit is that a person begins to glorify God and as he or she does, tongues the person has never learned come up out of the innermost being of the person. It is an impartation of the Holy Spirit. Jesus Christ Himself is the Baptizer and uses a Spirit filled willing vessel to flow through the vessel to a person such as copper wiring is used as a conduit for the flow of current.

Also, spiritual gifts can be imparted by the laying on of hands. An example of this is Where Moses lays hands on Joshua according to the commandment of God.

Numbers 27: 18 The Lord said to Moses, "Take Joshua the son of Nun, a man in whom is the Spirit, and lay your hand on him, 19 and cause him to stand before Eleazar the priest and before all the assembly, and command in their sight. 20 You will put some of your majesty on him, in order that all the assembly of the children of Israel will listen. 21 He will stand before Eleazar the priest, who will ask for him about the judgment of the Urim before the Lord. At his word will they go out, and at his word they will come in, both he and all the children of Israel with him, even all the assembly."

It is God who instructs Moses on what to do. God explains the transference of spirit to spirit. God promises to impart some of the anointing of Moses onto Joshua. Moses prays for Joshua to have wisdom and strength to lead Israel. It is done publicly with the approval of the priests. It is not only a transference but it shows the people of Israel what God is doing. God clearly chooses the successor to Moses. Moses did not decide by himself. The people see the results of obedience to God. What it does is build their faith and trust in Joshua. The results are that all of Joshua`s life, the people of Israel followed God and obeyed Joshua as a leader of the people.

They keep their promise to follow Joshua as they had followed Moses.

Joshua 1: 16 They answered Joshua, "All that you command us we will do, and wherever you send us we will go. 17 Just as we obeyed Moses in all things, we will obey you. May the Lord your God be with you, as He was with Moses! 18 Whoever rebels against your command and disobeys your words, in all that you command him, shall be put to death. Only be strong and courageous."

Joshua was not a stranger to the children of Israel. Joshua was close to Moses and was entrusted to help Moses. Joshua was mentored by Moses. The people of Israel knew him well. Moses, passes on gifts through the transference of spirit to spirit. The Bible says that a spirit of wisdom rested on Joshua because of it.

Barnabus and Saul

In this next instance the disciples were praying and someone prophesied that Barnabus and Saul should be separated unto God for ministry.

Acts 13: 2 As they worshipped the Lord and fasted, the Holy Spirit said, "Set apart for Me Barnabas and Saul for the work to which I have called them." 3 Then after fasting and praying, they laid their hands on them and sent them off.

Clearly it is not symbolic. The disciples prayed and fasted and laid hands and prayed. They seriously considered the action as sacred or holy. It is not simply a rite or an outward sign. It has significance. It is not a ritual. It is an expression of faith and an action done in faith so that God may use humans as vessels that He can pour His glory through.

It is an awesome thing to be sent by a church to minster. I have been a part of several churches where people were prayed for, sometimes prophesied over, and sent into ministry as missionaries or released into specific ministries locally. I was a part of a church who often prayed over prayer teams who would go pray throughout the city as they walked and prayed and believed God would pour out his Spirit in that area. Sometimes, they would evangelize on the street. Sometimes they would go just before the evening movie was to start. They would pray for anyone in the long ups.

Sometimes, they would preach to those in the long lines ups to popular bars on a Friday or Saturday. Other times, they would walk and pray claiming souls. Literally, the church would be praying and the pastors and elders would lay hands on us and pray that God would use us to pray and evangelize so that Christ would be magnified. They prayed for success but also anointing us with their authority and the church's authority to accomplish what we were sent to do.

Ritual or Sacrament

A ritual is something people do but it doesn't necessarily have any power to it. For instance, lighting a candle is something people do as part of worship in many denominations. Its meaning is symbolic only. It had meaning in the Old Testament because God instructed the priests to do it. Bowing one's head to pray is also a ritual. Many people observe it. The Bible doesn't say to bow your head and pray. The opposite is true. The Psalmist tells us to lift up our heads to praise God (Psalm 24: 9).

Laying on of hands is not just a religious rite. If you are only completing a ceremony with no faith – there is no sacrament only ritual. The difference between faith filled believers laying hands believing and imparting to believers and those just doing a ritual is huge. It is important that laying on of hands be practiced with faith because it is one of the fundamental doctrines of the Christian Church.

Don't believe that the laying on of hands without faith will accomplish anything. Also, don't elevate the laying on of hands of be something it is not. There are certain places it is used. It is not used for everything. Don't believe that you must receive by laying on of hands. It's one way of receiving. I want to give an example of receiving by faith but still receiving.

Never be Religious

To me, religious means- it must be this way and God can't do it any other way; I never want to be religious. God can use all kinds of ways to impart to people and to inspire or release people. Years ago, there was a special Evangelist who was preaching at my church during a youth convention. He would evangelize every person he met. He was passionate about reaching souls for Christ. He was inviting us to give our lives radically to God whatever it involved.

As he gave that altar call, I almost ran forward. I felt so strongly that he was personally speaking right into my spirit. I received that call to give myself to Christ wholly. About 1,500 people pressed towards the altar. There wasn't enough room. People were lined up all up and down the aisles of the church.

He was laying hands on some people and praying loudly into the microphone. I was receiving every word he spoke. I was yielding myself to God. I wish I could say he came and laid hands on me – but there were too many people. That doesn`t mean I didn't receive something. In fact, I believe, that day, I received a passion for the great commission. It was at that altar I received the baptism of the Holy Spirit as well – with no one laying hands on me. I received whatever God had for me, as much of God as God would give me. I received by faith in God. Never become religious and think, since there was no laying on of hands, nothing happened.

Discipleship and Mentoring

An example of where laying on of hands could be significant could be in a modern church someone is teaching a Bible class and gets an assistant to help him or her. The person trains the assistant so he or she knows what to do, how to do it etc. This exact thing occurred in my life. I was a recent convert, saved about one year. I had been in Bible class with a man nickname Skip and his wife, Polly. They instructed me, poured into me, loved me and were important in my life because I was the only Christian in my family. After the Bible class was over, I wanted to say good bye but it was hard for me. As I started to speak about the end of the semester, Polly, spoke up and said: We want you to come to the next class. I was relieved. I would still get to see them They had become spiritual parents to me. After the second class was complete, Polly approached me and asked me to stay on to help with the class. They got me to help take attendance, get materials, collect money, pray, lead in prayer etc. It was a learning experience because not only was I getting the Bible teaching but I was learning new ways of doing things and soaking up much of the passion for God both Skip and Polly had for God.

What happened is that I became a Bible teacher. I learned how to train others. I have had opportunity both to teach and also to train others for teaching. Imparting of an anointing or mentoring is not with every person you meet. You do it with someone you can spot the gifts in and or someone that God tugs at your heart to train. Not everyone can learn best from me. There is a chemistry between the mentor and the trainee. There is a smooth supernatural relationship where the person is trained and desires to learn all he or she can. You don`t do it casually. You do it prayerfully whether you are the mentor or the trainee. You believe it is God`s best and you give your best effort.

The Bible specifically warns us not to do it casually. It should be done with faith and prayerfully and for a specific purpose. Also, never let just anyone lay hands on you. Guard over this sacrament. Don`t regard it as casual. For example, there may be a class of 70 students; you may notice one or two individuals that have teaching gifts. It is those you should consider on training. It doesn`t mean you care less amount the others. It simply means you are to teach them but perhaps teaching isn`t their main gifting. Someone else should mentor them in some other area of gifting. The Holy Spirit will use us and speak to us about the individuals. The Holy Spirit will prompt us to invest in those individuals.

1 Timothy 5: 22 Do not lay hands suddenly on anyone, and do not partake of other men's sins. Keep yourself pure.

Also, you don't lay hands and pray for just anyone. As an altar prayer worker, I`ve had the opportunity to pray for hundreds of people who come to the altar for prayer. I would either hold the person`s hand or touch the person on the shoulder or forehead. The people come forward for the purposes of prayer. It was done properly. Should I be mentoring someone, God will quicken to me what to do. My relationship with God is most important. I believe in divine associations. That is, God bring the people; God releases the gift; God instructs about the laying on of hands. It is all Holy Spirit lead. You should never just let anyone lay hands on you and you just never just lay hands on anyone. The reason is because there is an impartation and you don`t just impart to anyone nor do you want just anyone imparting into your life.

Laying on of Hands to Impart a Blessing

The laying on of hands was used by patriarchs in the Old Testament to pronounce generational inherited blessings over the children. In this passage. Jacob, who God called Israel, is praying a blessing on Joseph`s sons Ephraim and Manasseh. He places his right hand on the youngest and his left hand on the oldest. This was not the way blessing were given. Usually, the first born would be prayed for with the right hand on him. Joseph tries to correct Israel but Israel says it is God`s choice not his own. He proclaims the larger blessing on the youngest one.

Genesis 48: 14 Israel stretched out his right hand and laid it on Ephraim's head, who was the younger, and his left hand on Manasseh's head, crossing his hands, for Manasseh was the firstborn.

15 He blessed Joseph and said,

"God, before whom my fathers
  Abraham and Isaac walked,

the God who fed me
   all my life long to this day,
16 the angel who redeemed me from all evil,
   bless the boys;
let them be called by my name,
   and the name of my fathers, Abraham and Isaac;
and let them grow into a multitude
   in the midst of the earth."

17 When Joseph saw that his father laid his right hand on the head of Ephraim, it displeased him, and he took hold of his father's hand to remove it from Ephraim's head to Manasseh's head. 18 Joseph said to his father, "Not so, my father, for this one is the firstborn. Put your right hand on his head."

19 His father refused and said, "I know it, my son, I know it. He will also become a people, and he will also be great, but truly his younger brother will be greater than he, and his descendants will become a multitude of nations." 20 He blessed them that day, saying,

"By you Israel will bless, saying,
   'May God make you like Ephraim and Manasseh.' "

So he set Ephraim before Manasseh.

   Israel was about to die so he wanted to pass on the generational blessings of Abraham, Isaac and now Israel – to Joseph`s sons. It involved prayer and literal laying on of hands.

Laying on of Hands for Confirmation

   The opportunity to lay hands on a person to confirm and ground the person in the truths he or she has studied is an essential part of our Christian faith. After studying the doctrines of Christ or after completing elementary teaching on Christian foundations, the students should receive confirmation. I don't know how much this is practiced in the protestant church but it should be.

   After a nine-month study on the foundations of the Christian faith, we had a special part of the Church service where we went forward for confirmation prayer. The ministers laid their hands on us as we kneeled and they prayed blessings upon us and that we would be firmly rooted in Christ. They prayed that our faith would be strong and that God would quicken the things we had been taught to us so we could live our lives for Christ.

We should pray for those who have completed foundational teaching and pray that the participants would be established in the faith. We should pray blessing over them. It not only shows that we approve of their studies but that we (ministers prayed but so did the congregation) receive them and strengthen them in the Christian faith. It is not simply a ritual. There were specific prayers over the different candidates. The person who prayed over me also prophesied over me. It was the leading of the Holy Spirit to establish me in the truths of Christ. They prayed for us to have a firm, strong foundation so we would only build on Christ as our foundation.

Jesus laid hands on the Children Imparting a Blessing.

Jesus purposely imparted a blessing on children This was not a mere love for children or an outward sign. It was to impart a blessing. Children were not often considered important but Jesus showed their value by choosing them and using them as an example of simple, true faith.

Matthew 19: 13 Then little children were brought to Him that He might put His hands on them and pray. But the disciples rebuked them.

14 But Jesus said, "Let the little children come to Me, and do not forbid them. For to such belongs the kingdom of heaven." 15 He laid His hands on them and departed from there.

Mark 10: 15 Truly I say to you, whoever does not receive the kingdom of God as a little child shall not enter it." 16 And He took them up in His arms, put His hands on them, and blessed them.

If you are a parent, or have children in your life at all, pray for them. Pray God's blessing on them, protection as well as that they would come to live pleasing lives to God. I believe that parenting is an important responsibility and an awesome privilege because you have been entrusted to care for them; spiritually you are the covering over the younger children until they can choose to live for Christ themselves.

My mother not only prayed for us as children but with her grandchildren, she would pray blessings over them each time she bathed them or they came to sit with her. It is a way of passing on a generational blessing of faith. It was especially important because I do not believe the parents prayed for their children. My mother prayed for them; I prayed for them and taught them Bible stories. I invested what I could into those who were in my life.

The Elders and Ministers

Part of what should be occurring in a Church service is that the elders and ministers should be laying hands on people who want a blessing. After I had first become a Christian, I went to every alter call for several years. I would pray about all thing in my life and give myself to God continuously. I have received many blessings by being quick to get prayer. I was the first Christian in my family so the prayers of those people were special to me. I had a Church family that prayed for me. Later, I became a prayer altar worker so that I could pray with others. I delighted in praying over people who came because I knew what God had done for me and believed He could also meet their needs.

Laying on of Hands for Ordination and Separation for Ministry

In Acts 13, Barnabus and Saul are separated for ministry together. The church prayed blessings and protection over them as they were sent out as missionaries. As a pastor or minister is dedicated to the service of God, Other ministers and elders lay hands on them separating them unto God for life long service. The person giving his or her life to serve God in ministry is giving wholly, spirit, soul and body to Jesus Christ for ministry. The ministers praying over them agree and often prophesies come forth because of the faith present.

Laying on of hands for Prophesy

1 Timothy 1: 18 This command I commit to you, my son Timothy, according to the prophecies that were previously given to you, that by them you might fight a good fight, 19 keeping faith and a good conscience, which some have rejected and suffered shipwreck in regard to their faith. 20

The Apostle Paul is reminding Timothy of the prophecies spoken over him. This type of friend is a treasure. A true godly friend will remind you of what God says about you and what prophecies you have received as promises of God. We should continuously remind God of what He has promised us, thanking Him for it and receiving it by faith even before we see a natural manifestation of it.

The gifts of the Spirit can be released in a person by laying hands on that person and prophesying and praying in faith. There should be elders and pastors who flow in the prophetic. Apostles and Prophets are usually the ones who get the prophetic words over people but it could come from any of the five-fold ministry. Our part is to receive in faith and stir up the giftings with our prayers and with our words. We can receive callings on God on our life through the laying on of hands with prophesy. What occurs is that something that wasn`t clear suddenly becomes clear and important as the known will of God for your life. Usually, it is a confirmation of something you already know about.

1 Timothy 4: 14 Do not neglect the gift that is in you, which was given to you by prophecy, with the laying on of hands by the elders.

Chapter questions

1. Did you receive specific prayer for impartation at the altar? Describe the event. Describe your own heart experience as well as the situation in chronological order.
2. Did you pray impartation over someone or more than one person? Describe it. What was the spiritual significance?
3. In your church do they pray impartation prayers over the congregation, the leadership, the pastors? Why?

7 RECEIVING IMPARTATION FOR MINISTRY

Receiving prophetic ministry the team ministering are apostles, prophets , other pastors. They confirm teachings and accomplishments as well as minister in scriptural prophetic prayer.

1 Tim 4: [14] Neglect not the gift that is in thee, which was given thee by prophecy, with the laying on of the hands of the presbytery.

[15] Meditate upon these things; give thyself wholly to them; that thy profiting may appear to all.

[16] Take heed unto thyself, and unto the doctrine; continue in them: for in doing this thou shalt both save thyself, and them that hear thee.

 2 Tim 2: [15] Study to shew thyself approved unto God, a workman that needeth not to be ashamed, rightly dividing the word of truth.

Literally, write the prophecies for yourself and pray them. Say out loud "God I receive this calling…" Literally come into agreement with the prophetic word over your life so that you see it spiritually. Start thanking God for it. Ask the Holy Spirit to direct your steps, and lead you and bring godly doors of opportunity in your life so that you might fulfill the Word of God concerning your life.

Minister's Candidate school

After three years of studying for ministry, we were to receive the laying on of hands with prophesy. My pastor was a strong prophet of God who usually prayed over all the graduates and prophesied over them, In my class, he did not do it as usual. He delayed it for a year. He gathered together several known prophets of God who would all lay hands on us and prophesy over us. This was something I longed for. It was the culmination of my studies. It meant a blessing over my life. I fasted. Please know this is a big deal for me. Fasting and prayer should be a part of our Christian lifestyle, but it comes easier to some than others. I was so expectant of what God would say about me through the prophets. I was also nervous. I kept in prayer all the way to church and the service itself was charged with an atmosphere of faith for the prophetic. Gathering the prophets is a special atmosphere. If you have not experienced it, I highly recommend you get into a true prophet of God`s service.

There is a special atmosphere for receiving miracles from God. I had studied three years of ministry classes, given myself to prayer and to serving in the Church. I wanted that special blessing that would come believing God would use those ministers to speak words of blessing over me.

In our graduating class, the ministers called each one of us up to the altar and we kneeled as the different prophets prayed and prophesied over us. They recorded each person`s prophetic word so that we could remember and as proof so we could know what to pray for. I highly recommend that you get a tape or a cd or mp3 of the prophecy as proof not only for your own self but as proof against any lie that may try to rise against it. I have kept those prophecies throughout the years and treasured them. I prayed them. I thank God for them. They have been like a compass to help me understand the seasons and help me to follow Christ.

Not just any person should lay hands on you. It should be somebody you respect, somebody you know, somebody who is true and sincere; the motives of the person`s heart matter. God will use prophets and apostles of God to prophesy and pray over those who believe to receive from the laying on of hands with prophesy. Faith is a key ingredient on your part and on the ministry team`s part.

Ordination – pastors – elders deacons consecrated for service

Those receiving promotion of authority in the Church receive impartation and conversation prayer from Apostle, pastors, and other ministers.

1 Timothy 1-16 is a New Testament example of requirements of those serving in ministry. It is the instruction of the Apostle Paul who started many churches and wrote some of our New Testament. His direction is to his spiritual son Timothy – but is meant for all the Church. It is a way of keeping order, spiritual purity, true Christian doctrine. There are strict guidelines as to the behaviour and lifestyle of Christians separating themselves for Christian leadership. Those who are promoted in the Church into positions of deacons and elders, those ordained for ministry or exhorter's papers are required to live lives above reproach. Although they may have many gifts of the Spirit, strong charismatic appeal, if they do not live lives that are morally pure, they cannot be considered for leadership.

The characteristics include hospitality, being transparent or the same in church as in regular life. It means literally believing in and living the scriptures. Being friendly and entertaining people to communicate Christ and to encourage Christians, should be part of their lifestyle. The ability to teach [God's Word] is essential as they will be required to share God's Word at their level of authority whether it be serving Communion, praying with someone, preaching or teaching.

1 Timothy 3 King James Version (KJV)
3 This is a true saying, if a man desire the office of a bishop, he desireth a good work.

[2] A bishop then must be blameless, the husband of one wife, vigilant, sober, of good behaviour, given to hospitality, apt to teach;

Personal characteristics of the candidate include he or she not be a drunkard. There are some Churches that forbid the drinking of alcohol. Those separated for ministry there, must abide by the calling. There are some churches that literally adhere to the scripture Gal 5: 21 – [not] "drunkenness" (Bible Gateway). Some Churches allow social drinking but forbid drunkenness. You must know and keep the rules of your church or it is sin for you to not obey them once a member or consecrated for ministry.

[3] Not given to wine, no striker, not greedy of filthy lucre; but patient, not a brawler, not covetous;

The person's character must include peace and friendliness – not a person getting into physical fights or verbal ones. He or she must be honest and not steal. This includes minor things that many people do not consider wrong such as taking stuff from your workplace for personal use at home. The person cannot be covetous – or desirous of someone else's possessions. It is a commandment. God gave these commandments to Moses. The List of qualities are in keeping with the commandments of God.

Patience (Gal 5: 23) is a fruit of godly character. Rather than being one offended or one to cause strife, the person should be temperate, gentle, kind, humble. Although the minister must use spiritual gifts to effectively do his or her ministry, character is the thing most emphasized in the scriptures. Why? Godly character, true Christian adherence to the scriptures is the only way the true gospel can be shared or passed on. Mary Alice Isleib, an excellent preacher, said " The power of our gospel is the purity of our gospel". Our Saviour set the example of godly character and we are to live believing in the scriptures without sin. If we sin, there should be immediate repentance. If it is a sin that shames the gospel such as public drunkenness, the minister will be reproved. If it is a sexual sin, the person may be reproved or dismissed if there is no repentance.

The requirements include the family unit. The minister's children should be living lives as examples of Christ. The Christian family model is emphasized as the raising of children honouring their parents, honouring God is emphasized.

[4] One that ruleth well his own house, having his children in subjection with all gravity;

[5] (For if a man know not how to rule his own house, how shall he take care of the church of God?)

A new Christian is often very passionate for Christ and will share Christ with every person he or she meets. The truth is he or she would give testimony and preach from the pulpit should we let them. I've known of people who have had radical salvation experiences, I myself being one. The truth was I was so passionate about Christ, I witnessed to every person I met. Also, the truth was I had not yet studied the scriptures or doctrines of Christ so I could share the salvation message and not much more. I was entrusted to share my testimony publicly. I was honoured to speak in the Church but I didn't preach. The Scriptures warn us against promoting a new believer who is zealous but lacks scriptural knowledge.

[6] Not a novice, lest being lifted up with pride he fall into the condemnation of the devil.

There is a warning concerning pride. Although this scripture can apply to those not mature. Pride or self exaltation can apply to seasoned ministers also. It is necessary that ministry remain accountable to God, to each other, to their spouses etc. If a person believes he or she is an exception to the commandments of God – the person is in sin. Should there be immediate repentance, it would be resolved. If not, the person is living dangerously. It is essential that we pray for our leaders that God would keep and protect them.

It is interesting that the quality of the person's life in the community is also essential to ministry opportunity. His or her reputation within the community, in the workplace etc. should be the same as in the Church. There is no double life. A double life is someone living a model Christian life on Sundays and church days but not consistently in all his or her life.

[7] Moreover he must have a good report of them which are without; lest he fall into reproach and the snare of the devil.

Deacons and elders assist the pastors in various functions within the church. Some churches only have elders and one elder, or more are the main shepherds of the church. In the churches of my experience in the

Charismatic, Pentecostal, four square, full gospel circles, there are pastors consecrated to different aspects of preaching, teaching and departments within the church. The elders and deacons are proven with the similar criteria as the ministry team. They will minister sacraments, prayer, visitation, assist with prayer at the altar, and other aspects to assist the ministry team.

These leaders [as should all of us] must be wise with their words. They should speak truth. They should speak words of encouragement, things that align with the Word of God. The things we say impact not only our own lives but also the lives of others.

8 Likewise must the deacons be grave, not double tongued, not given to much wine, not greedy of filthy lucre;

This scripture means living a pure Christian life.

9 Holding the mystery of the faith in a pure conscience.

10 And let these also first be proved; then let them use the office of a deacon, being found blameless.

11 Even so must their wives be grave, not slanderers, sober, faithful in all things.

12 Let the deacons be the husbands of one wife, ruling their children and their own houses well.

Deacons are the servant leaders who minister sacraments, organize cell groups. They are generally very friendly and devoted to their ministry. They interact with all types of people and serve them as though serving Christ.

13 For they that have used the office of a deacon well purchase to themselves a good degree, and great boldness in the faith which is in Christ Jesus.

14 These things write I unto thee, hoping to come unto thee shortly:

The Apostle Paul reverences God and realizes Christ's passion for the Church. The Church must be a spotless Bride for Christ. The Church must be without sin (Ephesians 5: 25-28).

15 But if I tarry long, that thou mayest know how thou oughtest to behave thyself in the house of God, which is the church of the living God, the pillar and ground of the truth.

[16] And without controversy great is the mystery of godliness: God was manifest in the flesh, justified in the Spirit, seen of angels, preached unto the Gentiles, believed on in the world, received up into glory.

Chapter questions

1. Did you witness the ordination or impartation of someone or more than one for ministry? Describe it.
2. What was your response during and after?
3. If you did not witness someone's ordination – examine the chapter criteria for ministry and write your expression of why these things are important for a minister.

8 THE ALTARS ARE FOR THE CHURCH

The ministry teams at the altar are self prayer, and/or pastors, deacons, elders and altar workers.

The altar area is an excellent place for preservice prayer. Should all the church members attend, they can join hands and encircle the inside of the church sanctuary. They can pray for the service, for the presence of the Holy Spirit to be released n them, that the worship would be an offering to God, that the Word would be received by the congregation, that the minister would preach with God's anointing. (usually no more than 10-15 minutes) There should be a prayer room with longer for individual and/ or group prayer before the meeting (30 min – 1hour) but all the church joining in prayer to begin the service is a special way to begin. I am not advocating that it occur each week, only that it should occur as an option.

I've been a part of a Church where we would worship; and the pastor had a discerning anointing for the body of the congregation and would give an altar call as soon as he was on the platform. It impacted all of the Church – often everyone went forward. It was not each gathering but it occurred, and the results were accurate – the congregation responded accordingly. During these altar calls, we would individually pray and corporately pray.

After a prophetic Word

The gift of prophecy is for the building up of the church. Often after a prophetic Word has been given there will be a response by the congregation. A pastor may speak the words that we respond to the prophetic word by praying accepting it or applying it. Either all the congregation responds or occasionally there are specific types of people indicated who respond. It may be moving to the altar area at the front. In many large church services, the altar call overspills into the aisles and throughout the first floor of the sanctuary. It is a specific response to a Word for the Church.

Luke 8: 8 And other fell on good ground, and sprang up, and bare fruit an hundredfold. And when he had said these things, he cried, He that hath ears to hear, let him hear.

Altar calls after a preached sermon

Often the Word of God compels us to respond. There should be a self examination with invitation to receive prayer each week after every sermon. There may be many or not many who respond. In most churches, should the Word pierce the hearts of the people, it will compel the people to prayer.

Luke 8: 15 But that on the good ground are they, which in an honest and good heart, having heard the word, keep it, and bring forth fruit with patience

I've been in some Church services where the minister will instruct the congregation to kneel and pray at their seats, making an altar of their seat. It has often been a person application of the Word that was preached that I received as truth. It has often been life changing. Some of my most life changing prayer occurred as we were given an altar call and we could linger in prayer as long as desired.

There should always be an altar call at the end of each service whether it be general or specific. A specific one will draw those people. For instance, in my present Church, there is always an altar call for teachers and students upon return to school September). A general altar call may offer prayer for salvation, healing /deliverance, or special requests. There are always Christians who desire the prayer of agreement.

Matthew 18: 19 Again I say unto you, That if two of you shall agree on earth as touching any thing that they shall ask, it shall be done for them of my Father which is in heaven.

20 For where two or three are gathered together in my name, there am I in the midst of them.

Consecration – separation of yourself – rededications – special vows Receiving God's Word – with prayer, praise 2 Tim 3: 14-16, Eph 5:26, Joshua 24:15

There are almost always visitors or teens or children who may want prayer to receive Christ as Saviour. There may be recommitment to Christ or some other situation. The offering of prayer at the altar is a necessary aspect of our ministry as a Church.

Funerals – last Christian gathering to honour a life

Death was not God's plan for humans. It was the consequence of disobedience to God's commandment not to eat from a certain tree in the garden. They could enjoy the fruits from all the other trees, shrubs etc. The consequences of eating from it meant death not only for Adam and Eve but all humans that would ever live. The ritual of burying the deceased began with the death of Abel murdered by his brother. The belief of Pharisees (Judaism) was that the souls of the righteous were in Abraham's Bosom in the center of the earth. Abraham was a righteous man. He was an idol worshipper but God spoke to him and Abraham obeyed. Through his obedience the nation of Israel began. One part of the center of the earth was for the righteous; the other part was Sheol Hades – a place of torment. All who died would stay there until the resurrection of the dead on judgement day.

Genesis 3: 3 But of the fruit of the tree which is in the midst of the garden, God hath said, Ye shall not eat of it, neither shall ye touch it, lest ye die.[19] In the sweat of thy face shalt thou eat bread, till thou return unto the ground; for out of it wast thou taken: for dust thou art, and unto dust shalt thou return.

Jesus speaks of the consequences of living a righteous life on earth and the consequences of living selfishly sinfully.

Luke 16: 22 And it came to pass, that the beggar died, and was carried by the angels into Abraham's bosom: the rich man also died, and was buried;

23 And in hell he lift up his eyes, being in torments, and seeth Abraham afar off, and Lazarus in his bosom.

24 And he cried and said, Father Abraham, have mercy on me, and send Lazarus, that he may dip the tip of his finger in water, and cool my tongue; for I am tormented in this flame.

25 But Abraham said, Son, remember that thou in thy lifetime receivedst thy good things, and likewise Lazarus evil things: but now he is comforted, and thou art tormented.

26 And beside all this, between us and you there is a great gulf fixed: so that they which would pass from hence to you cannot; neither can they pass to us, that would come from thence.

Jesus Christ suffered, died and was buried. He descended into the Bosom of Abraham but he also plundered hell – by preaching and taking authority over all living and dead by his righteous offering – his blood for our lives. After the resurrection of Jesus – he ascended into heaven. No longer do the righteous who believe in Jesus descend into Abraham's Bosom. Once the righteous die, they are in the presence of Jesus Christ in heaven. Judgement day has not occurred yet. It will be the last day. It is the end of the earth as we know it. All living and dead shall appear at the throne of Christ. They will be judged on whether or not they accepted Christ as Saviour. Those who did not accept Christ, will appear at the White Throne Judgement – where they will be sentenced, condemned to be separated from God all of eternity. Rev 20: 4-5, Rev 20: 11-14

Matthew 25: [31] When the Son of man shall come in his glory, and all the holy angels with him, then shall he sit upon the throne of his glory:

[32] And before him shall be gathered all nations: and he shall separate them one from another, as a shepherd divideth his sheep from the goats:

[33] And he shall set the sheep on his right hand, but the goats on the left.

[34] Then shall the King say unto them on his right hand, Come, ye blessed of my Father, inherit the kingdom prepared for you from the foundation of the world:

[35] For I was an hungred, and ye gave me meat: I was thirsty, and ye gave me drink: I was a stranger, and ye took me in:

[36] Naked, and ye clothed me: I was sick, and ye visited me: I was in prison, and ye came unto me.

[37] Then shall the righteous answer him, saying, Lord, when saw we thee an hungred, and fed thee? or thirsty, and gave thee drink?

[38] When saw we thee a stranger, and took thee in? or naked, and clothed thee?

[39] Or when saw we thee sick, or in prison, and came unto thee?

[40] And the King shall answer and say unto them, Verily I say unto you, Inasmuch as ye have done it unto one of the least of these my brethren, ye have done it unto me.

Jesus words to the Apostle John in Revelation are concerning the Church. His coming is a warning for us to be ready which means to live uprightly –

keeping the commandments, living unselfishly, serving Christ with passion and zeal.

Rev 22: 12 [12] And, behold, I come quickly; and my reward is with me, to give every man according as his work.

At a Christian funeral, there will be some rejoicing; there shall be some celebration of the person's life. It is unlike funerals of those who do not know Christ. There is sorrow but it is overshadowed by the joy of knowing the loved one is in the presence of Christ.

There are posted pictures from the person's life, life accomplishments such as awards on display, worship songs, speeches given by those who were closest to the person, as well as brief speeches given by others. The tradition in a Christian funeral is to place the body at the front of the church in the altar.

In Charismatic, Pentecostal, four square, full gospel churches, we do not pray for the dead. We pray for the family and loved ones. We respect the body of the person but realize it is not the essence of the person – it is the shell of the person. Once the body dies, the Christian's soul rises to Christ.

Should there be attendees who do not know Christ, they will witness a unique type of funeral. Sometimes there is an exhortation by the pastor or a speaker to the audience to examine their hearts, so they know Jesus as Saviour. It may be a scripture or a prayer – but it is essential as there may be people there who might not get in a church any other way.

Chapter questions
1. Describe the importance of an "altar experience" in your own life. In your church.
2. Is there a physical altar structure in your church? Is it necessary or unnecessary? Explain.
3. Describe a typical month at your church. What altar experiences are you a part of or are witnessing?

9 DESTINY DECISIONS

There are special occasions when the congregation is choosing Christ in Destiny decisions. The ministry team includes yourself (praying for yourself). Apostles, Prophets, Evangelists, Pastors, Teachers, Elders, Deacons as well as altar workers.

The altar is for Destiny decisions – preaching God's Word can impart faith for life decisions. Pastors, Teachers, Evangelists, Prophets, Apostles – the ministry are accountable not only to the churches they are preaching in but especially accountable to God. Those who seriously pray and preach or present the gospel keeping their lives pure will be judged by Christ with rewards such as a crown. Those who abuse the authority of the pulpit to the congregation will be judged most severely by Christ. The congregation depends on words of life coming from the leaders. Those words can encourage, exhort, persuade. The ministry should be to build up, encourage and strengthen the saints directing them to seek Christ. The altar calls are places where people pray over life changing things. The choices are eternal.

The altar calls present the congregation with an opportunity to choose between a deeper relationship with Christ in some way. I'm not saying that if you don't go to every altar call you are not obeying God. Each sermon, each presentation of God's Word, even the reading of scripture is an opportunity to believe and draw closer to God. We should examine our hearts, so we have no sin or hard spot in it. You will know if there is by the Word of God preached or studied. The Holy Spirit inspired the writers of the Scriptures and the Word of God is living. It speaks to us who are Christians. The anointed preached word is a way for us to examine our hearts. The attitude of a Christian with God is not passive but active. We are in the present seeking His direction and absorbing His truth.

Joshua warns the Israelites after the death of Moses, that they must continue serving God. He recounts the miracles God did by delivering them our of slavery in Egypt and providing for them for 40 years in the wilderness bringing them into the new land – the same land God promised to Abraham.

Eternal CHOICES

Genesis 26: [3] Sojourn in this land, and I will be with thee, and will bless thee; for unto thee, and unto thy seed, I will give all these countries, and I will perform the oath which I sware unto Abraham thy father;

⁴ And I will make thy seed to multiply as the stars of heaven, and will give unto thy seed all these countries; and in thy seed shall all the nations of the earth be blessed;

Joshua 24: ¹⁵ And if it seem evil unto you to serve the LORD, choose you this day whom ye will serve; whether the gods which your fathers served that were on the other side of the flood, or the gods of the Amorites, in whose land ye dwell: but as for me and my house, we will serve the LORD.

Jesus on his entry into Jerusalem on Palm Sunday was to be a day of victory, people shouting "Hosanna" and Israel welcoming him. In preparation for his entry, he chose a donkey a colt (in fulfillment of Messianic prophecy). He instructed the disciples to get the donkey from a place where two ways meet. The place of two ways is a place of destiny decision. That donkey, that colt was serving a purpose – there is more than one use for his life though. He was chosen by Jesus to enter Jerusalem. Jesus spoke and said if anyone asked why the disciples were taking him to say "the Master requires him". His word was enough to secure that specific donkey. The donkey had served an ordinary purpose until that day. He was an ordinary donkey but he was chosen making his life significant.

Mark 11: ⁴ And they went their way, and found the colt tied by the door without in a place where two ways met; and they loose him.

As that donkey was at a place of two ways, many people who come to the church congregation are in a place of making destiny decisions. The preaching of God's Word can release a supernatural calling or direction in the hearts of the people. At the altar the people may commit their lives to Christ in a fresh new way. They may make decisions that direct them in new ways.

I myself made a destiny decision at an altar such as that. I was a new Christian – less than a year – The Evangelist guest minister had preached so that each word he spoke was emphasized in my soul. When he gave the altar call for people to give their lives to Christ whether it meant going to a different country to preach, to preach the gospel or to die for Christ, I almost ran to the altar. I knew it was my decision to live for Christ beyond what I knew. I couldn't get close top the altar because it was filled with at least a thousand people. I got as close as I could. As he was praying over us,

I was praying yielding all my spirit, soul, body to Christ – in a fresh way – beyond what I had known. Suddenly I began praising God and speaking in tongues. I did not know what speaking in tongues was. I had had no teaching. I wasn't scared because I knew it was God's presence. I continued worshipping. After I got back to my seat I asked the woman who had brought me what it is – speaking in other languages I hadn't learned and she read the scripture to me; she assured me it was an experience from God. I made the decision to yield my life as a minister of the gospel.

Destiny decisions of the type of speaking of (becoming a minister of the gospel) occur often at church altar calls. The calling of the Apostle Elisha to serve and honour God was not at an altar call, but the elements of an altar call were there. Elijah the prophet, approached Elisha and cast his mantle upon him. His mantle was authority as a prophet. It was a symbolic but direct invitation to become his trainee. Elisha was torn. He wanted to go with the prophet but he wanted to pay his respects to his parents. He was at a place of life changing decision. He was ploughing the earth, busy with natural work but called to specific use by God through the prophet Elijah. The result of his decision is that he slew the oxen and made a huge meal. He left all he knew and followed Elijah who trained him as a prophet.

1 Kings 19: [19] So he departed thence, and found Elisha the son of Shaphat, who was plowing with twelve yoke of oxen before him, and with the twelfth: and Elijah passed by him, and cast his mantle upon him.

[20] And he left the oxen, and ran after Elijah, and said, Let me, I pray thee, kiss my father and my mother, and then I will follow thee. And he said unto him, Go back again: for what have I done to thee?

[21] And he returned back from him, and took a yoke of oxen, and slew them, and boiled their flesh with the instruments of the oxen, and gave unto the people, and they did eat. Then he arose, and went after Elijah, and ministered unto him.

The miracles of Elijah and Elisha are throughout the Old Testament. The miracles were healing, multiplication miracles, resurrection of the dead etc. as well as preaching God's Word and speaking God's Word to kings and leaders.

Chapter End questions

1. List the altar life changing decisions you made.
2. Describe each of the decisions.
3. Explain what occurred in your life as a result of each of the decisions.

CONCLUSUION

HEART DECISIONS

The purpose for this book was to cause we, the Christian Charismatic Church, to examine the scriptures concerning the importance of the altar experience to us as a Church. It is my hope that you have examined your heart during the reading of the chapters and reflected on the chapter questions applying the scriptures to yourself. It is our experience with Christ in our churches, in our gatherings, in our homes that transforms us from glory to glory (1 Cor. 3: 18).

SECTION FOR PASTORS, MINISTRY TEAM

Of specific emphasis in the book, as in my heart are those who minister at the altars whether they are pastors, apostles, prophets, evangelists, teachers or elders or deacons or altar workers. Our prayerful ministry with impartation and with the prayer of agreement has eternal significance. It is necessary that we allow altar experiences and prioritize them so the congregation will respond. It may be a brief prayer. It may be a long prayer. Altar experiences are destiny decisions. Our offering of them is our part in the spiritual growth of the people we serve.

THE ALTAR IS A PRIORITY

Decision – Often the congregation is making decisions for life.
Importance – The congregation is recognizing important aspects of the Word of God preached.
Priority – We are prioritizing how God's Spirit is speaking to us.
Urgent – We must keep the altar calls as an important part of the message because it is what the congregation does with God's Word that determines spiritual growth. The Words without a heart response are words unfulfilled. We must emphasize the altar call – I mean we should offer prayer for salvation, healing, deliverance regularly. We should invite people to come for prayer emphasizing it is an occasion to apply the Word to their hearts, to apply the Word to their lives. It is an opportunity to connect with God and receive something of eternal significance.

EMPHASIS ON SELF EXAMINATION

It is my wish, my desire that you would consider the offering each altar call with the examination of your own heart spiritually, that you would not sit in your seat or leave when you feel a nudge of the Holy Spirit prompting you to respond spiritually. It can be a brief prayer, but it is the sealing of the Word in your heart and life that makes the difference. A Presentation of yourself spirit, soul and body (1 Thess. 5: 23) is the result of an altar call. A fresh consecration.

Pure – our heart motive should be pure – to connect with God receive from God.

Spiritual - Receive what God is offering through the preached WORD into your own heart.

Individual – Your individual needs can be met at the altar. God cares for all the congregation but as you respond to the altar call, you a receiving individual, specific ministry.

Serving the Church – As you receive from God, you can share with others how Christ has transformed your life. You can become an altar worker praying for others.

Honouring God – The main purpose of the altar is to honour God – to connect with the Spirit – to give our offering of our lives, to receive his anointing that engrafts the Word of God into our hearts. The altar is the attitude of the heart – it is the opportunity to receive the life of God in an instance.

PRAYERS

PRAYERS

PRAYERS   The following prayers are samples of prayers you could pray for important reasons. You could pray the same meaning in your own words. The prayers are meant as examples only.   PRAYER FOR SALVATION   Thank you- Jesus that you died for me on the cross. Thank you that you rose from the dead and ascended into heaven. Thank you that you are coming back again. I thank you Jesus for forgiving my sins. Thank you for your blood that cleanses me from all sin and unrighteousness. Thank you that your blood makes me holy. Thank you for saving me. Fill me with the Holy Spirit to overflowing. I pray for the baptism of the Holy Spirit. Lead me to other people who love you and serve you and that can help me know more about you. Give me the discerning of spirits strong. I thank you and praise you. With my mouth, I confess Jesus Christ is my LORD. Amen.

PRAYER FOR BAPTISM OF THE HOLY SPIRIT   Thank you- Jesus that you promised to send the gift of the Holy Spirit to us. Thank you that this promise is to all believers. I am a believer. I want all of you that you will give me. I want to know you God. Baptize me in the Holy Spirit with the evidence of speaking in other tongues. I believe you want to fill me to overflowing with your Spirit so that I might be an effective witness for Christ on the earth. Thank you for saving me. Thank you for your Holy presence. [begin praising God for what He has done for you – sing worship choruses and praise God in your natural language. Believe that He is present with you – start praising and worshipping Him. As phrases come to you in other tongues, say them – praise God with new tongues.] I praise you. I thank you. I receive the baptism of the Holy Spirit.
Chris A. Legebow

PRAYER FOR RELEASING ANGELS   God, I thank you that angels are ministering spirits sent as ministers to us. I pray over my prayer request NAME IT HERE. God I pray release angels to perform it. I thank you for releasing the answer to me. I praise you for it. Amen.   PRAYER FOR

RESISTING EVIL   I am the redeemed of the LORD. Jesus Christ has saved me. I am a new creation in Christ Jesus. Jesus blood covers me. I live in the spirit. The Holy Spirit of God fills my spirit. O Holy Spirit quicken me; give me wisdom. Pray [expecting God will give you discerning of spirits so you will have the right words to speak.]   In the name of Jesus Christ, I bind you. I rebuke you evil spirit. In the name of Jesus, I command you to go out. You have no place in my life. I cast you out. You have no place with me. I am covered by the blood of Jesus and His righteousness is my righteousness. Go out evil spirit in the name of Jesus Christ!   Thank you, Holy Spirit for your holy presence. Release angels to drive out the enemy. Thank you. Amen.

 PRAYER FOR PROTECTION   Holy Spirit release angels to protect me. I plead the blood of Jesus over me. I pray the protection you promise to your people. Cover me Jesus. Holy Spirit give me wisdom, discernment and understanding. Thank you for angels that guard over me. Thank you for your blood that protects me and a hedge of protection around me. I praise you O God. [praise God with some worship choruses and expect God's holy presence to be manifest in you]. Thank you. O God for protection.

PRAYER FOR HEALING
Israel our Christian Heritage: Israel our Christian Destiny

Lord Jesus, thank you that you gave your life for me so that I can be saved, healed and delivered. I thank you for the scripture that by your stripes I am healed. I thank you for my healing.   NAME THE DISEASE I bind you in the name of Jesus. I cast you out. I pray over myself that I would be whole spirit, soul and body.   Thank you, God. for your healing manifestation in my life. I give you all the glory. Amen.

PRAYER OF REPENTENCE   Jesus, thank you for your blood shed for me. I repent of the sin of NAME IT. I thank you for liberty from sin. I cut off the root of iniquity in my family. I thank you for your empowering presence to live a Holy life. Holy Spirit lead and guide me in the paths of righteousness. Thank you for giving me godly desires. Let my life align with your word. In Jesus name. Amen.   Prayer of dedication as a giver   God, thank you for prospering me. Let me be a giver you can use to give to others. God let my character be humble and giving so that you place things and wealth in my hands, and I will give as you lead me. If you prosper me with more than enough, I will obey your promptings to give to the gospel, to people and for the glory of God. Use me as a giver. I give myself wholly to you. In Jesus name. Amen.

Prayer for Israel

God I pray for the peace of Jerusalem (Psalm 122: 6). I pray for all of Israel to be saved (Romans 11: 25). I pray for you to make Jerusalem a praise and a fame throughout all the earth. (Isaiah 62:7). I pray you will keep Israel as the apple of your eye and hide her under the shadow of your wing. (Psalm 17:8). I pray for the Word of God to be written in their hearts. (Jeremiah 31: 33; Ezekiel 11: 19) Reveal yourself as Jesus the Messiah to the people of Israel and Jewish people everywhere. Amen.

Of course, you can pray other things for the blessing of Israel. It is essential to pray scripture as God has made covenant with Israel.

ABOUT THE AUTHOR

Chris Legebow is a Christian Professor of English and Communications. She has taught at the elementary, high school and College and University levels. She has ministered in her local churches in intercessory prayer, teaching Sunday school and other Christian Doctrine classes to children and youth. She has preached to congregations and given her testimony. Although she was not raised in a Christian home, she came to know Jesus Christ as her Saviour and LORD while she was studying in University. This radically transformed her life in terms of priorities and commitment.

She has a strong passion for the great commission – that Jesus Christ would be preached throughout all the earth believing that it a major sign of the LORD's return. She has been a part of several different types of full gospel charismatic churches but has also gained much of her insight and enlightenment from Christian Media and broadcasting. She hopes to continue ministering, serving, interceding and giving and teaching until the LORD returns

OTHER BOOKS BY   CHRIS A. LEGEBOW
Available on Amazon.ca Amazon.com or Kindle

By Living Word Publishers
Angels: Ministering Spirits
The Christian Charismatic Church
Discipling the Generation
An Excellent Spirit:
Living Life Wholly Unto God
Covenant With God: God's Relationship With Man
Discovering and Using your Spiritual Gifts
Discipling The Generation
Divine Healing in the Scriptures: God's Mercy Towards Man
Israel Our Christian Heritage: Israel Our Christian Destiny
Jesus Christ: Saviour, Healer, Deliverer, LORD
Kinds of Giving: From the Holy Scriptures
Signs of Jesus Coming

Spheres of Authority: Know yours
The Commandments
The Doctrine of Christ: Essential Truths of Scripture
The Five-Fold Ministry: Gifts to the Church
Kinds of Prayer. Knowing Them and Using Them Effectively
Living Life Fully: Knowing your Purpose
The Anointing: The Glory of God
The Charismatic Christian Church
The High Calling: Life Worth Living
The High Life: Communion with the Holy Spirit
The Sacraments: A Charismatic Guide

www.ingramcontent.com/pod-product-compliance
Lightning Source LLC
Chambersburg PA
CBHW032048040426
42449CB00007B/1028